CREATIVE IDEAS FOR CHRISTMAS 1988

COMPILED AND EDITED BY
KATHLEEN ENGLISH AND ALISON NICHOLS

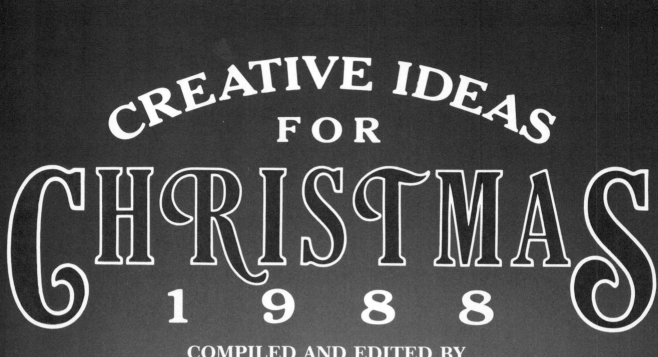

Oxmoor House®

Library of Congress Catalog Number: 84-63033
ISBN: 0-8487-0732-X
ISSN: 0883-9085
Manufactured in the United States of America
First Printing

Executive Editor: Candace N. Conard
Production Manager: Jerry Higdon
Associate Production Manager: Rick Litton
Art Director: Bob Nance

Creative Ideas for Christmas 1988

Senior Editor: Nancy Janice Fitzpatrick
Editors: Kathleen English, Alison Nichols
Editorial Assistants: Josie E. Lee, Jennifer Zanon
Production Assistant: Theresa L. Beste
Copy Chief: Mary Jean Haddin
Artists: Melissa M. Jones, Melinda P. Goode,
   Larry Hunter, Nancy Johnson
Senior Designer: Cynthia R. Cooper

Senior Foods Editor: Margaret Chason Agnew
Assistant Foods Editor: Laura Massey
Recipes tested by: Julie Fisher, Lisa Glass,
   Paula N. Saunders
Foods Editorial Assistant: Pam Beasley Bullock

To find out how you can order *Cooking Light* magazine, write to *Cooking Light®*, P.O. Box C-549, Birmingham, AL 35283

Contents

Continued

Continued

INTRODUCTION

Are you ready? The countdown is on for Christmas! It's time to prepare for the celebrations to come. Leaf through this book, and you'll find all you'll need to make Christmas 1988 the best ever.

HOME FOR THE HOLIDAYS

Christmas is a time of joy and sharing. It's a time of welcoming family and friends and declaring again the faith from which yuletide observations stem. Enjoy the unique ideas and talents of the very special people in this chapter, as they prepare to celebrate the season that enriches us all. Catch the enthusiasm they display and apply it to your own holiday endeavors.

Add a Note of Christmas

The use of musical instruments in holiday decorating can make a room sing with the harmony of the season. That approach was a natural for the living room of Steve and Normie Sanford, since Steve is a musician and school band director in Fredericksburg, Virginia. The trombone is Steve's forte, and he plays with various groups, including a "big band," which has raised over $500,000 for charity.

To help trim the Sanfords' tree for the Historic Foundation Tour, schoolchildren in art classes made colorful drums and fans. The rhythmic placement of ribbons, balls, and dried flowers added jazzy notes of pink, gold, and burgundy to the tree. A generous composition of magnolia crowned the grand piano in concert with its large scale. The handcrafted dulcimer performed in a showcase mantel arrangement, and even the music stand, garlanded in box-wood and ivy, added a festive beat.

Above: Nestled in a bed of cedar, boxwood, and pink statice on the Sanfords' mantel is a dulcimer made by a Tennessee craftsman. Reflected in the mirror, Richard peers over the banister.

Preceding pages: Normie Sanford and sons enjoy their lyrical Christmas decor. The children's father is the real musician, but when Dad's away, the boys will play. Richard, cheeks puffy with the effort, blasts away on the trombone while brothers (Will at the piano and Stephen in Mom's lap) cover their ears. The racket will, no doubt, awaken baby brother David from his afternoon nap.

Livable, Lovable Christmas Color

"I want to start playing carols on the first cool day of autumn, even on Halloween! I am a really big Christmas enthusiast, and those colors just appeal to me, especially the rich, hunter green," says Ann Evans, explaining the color scheme of her house—red, green, and white.

Although Ann and David Evans knew what colors they wanted to use in their house, they started out tentatively. At first

Below: Ann bought the wicker furniture new at a local hardware store for a good price. She spray-painted it green and then added a brown glaze to give it a patina. She knew she had succeeded in the effect when one gentleman on the tour observed, "Look at that antique wicker. You just don't see really good wicker like that any more." Ann added cushions and a tablecloth in a bold botanical print, and a braided rug to complete the inviting scene.

For holiday dress-up, the mantel is garbed in greenery, and a grapevine swan, encircled with tiny white lights, seems to float in the fireplace. A rustic bench holds a festive arrangement, and the tree, studded with balls and baby's breath, stands in a corner.

Above: Ann settled on her favorite gingerbread recipe because its spicy aroma lingers. She ties pungent gingerbread heart cookies to a branch with raffia and attaches the branch to the pine hutch, which is filled with her country collectibles.

they painted all walls and woodwork white, finished the floors in a natural stain, and added color in the stenciling only. Then they wanted more color, so they painted some woodwork here, a door there. When they got to the foyer, "I didn't think it was brave at all to paint the floor in red and white diamonds," says Ann.

The Evanses agreed to open their home to a holiday tour because, as Ann recalls, "It gave us a deadline to finish up all our work, and we needed it." (The house is just a few doors from the Sanford home, shown on the preceding pages, and was on the same tour in Fredericksburg, Virginia.)

Simple Christmas decorations—greenery, berries, cones, apples, and gingerbread shapes—in garlands, sprays, and spilling from baskets, suit the Evanses' furnishings. Visitors to this attractive setting may, like Ann, wish that Christmas lasted longer.

Above: This foyer makes a remarkable impression, and paint is the key. Baseboards, window casings, and parts of the staircase are painted green. The handrail and treads are finished so that their natural grain shows through, and the stair risers are papered in a red print. But the real drama is on the floor, checkered in big red and white diamonds. For a seasonal welcome, a thick garland of evergreen holly and hemlock, bejeweled with their respective berries and cones, wags its way down the stairs.

6

Partners in Herbs

If you believe in fate, then theirs was a pairing meant to be. But 16 years ago, all Barbara Steele and Marlene Lufriu knew of each other was what Barbara heard from the realtor selling Marlene and her husband land: that Barbara and Marlene would like being neighbors because they grew the same kind of funny plants. Those plants happened to be herbs, and the two women are now partners in a commercial enterprise called Alloway Gardens and Herb Farm. They operate out of a log cabin, where each year they hold a Christmas open house.

At the time the women met, Barbara Steele and her husband, Roger, owned part of an old farm in Littlestown, Pennsylvania, just a couple of miles from the Maryland border. The region is known for its excellent farmland, and it naturally followed that the two herb growers would make good use of the soil.

"Marlene came over one day with her husband, Ivan, and introduced herself," Barbara says. "She explained that she was with the Cylburn Arboretum in Baltimore. I had all these lamb's ear plants, and she said, if you would like to pot some of those and sell them wholesale at the Arboretum show, you could. I did, and those were the first plants that I ever sold. My big business!" she recalls with a laugh. "And I took all the money and invested it in more herb plants."

The two women planted a joint herb garden and were soon selling all they grew, so they began expanding. Now they offer about 200 varieties of plants, including flowers, herbs, and vegetables. With the help of their husbands, they put up a log cabin near Barbara's house to serve as their shop. They sell gardening supplies and crafts, along with the mainstay of herbs and flowers. They conduct workshops, give tours of their gardens, and have booths at farmers' markets, greens sales, and other functions. That way, they keep busy during

Above: Marlene, left, and Barbara, right, enjoy a break in the holiday rush with cups of coffee, muffins, and some of Marlene's herbed jellies. Below, she shares with us the recipe for her jelly that uses the herb, savory.

SAVORY HERB JELLY
¾ cup water
3 tablespoons dried savory
1 cup grapefruit juice
3½ cups sugar
1 pouch liquid Certo

Combine water and savory in a saucepan. Bring to a boil; cover, reduce heat, and simmer 10 minutes. Strain mixture, reserving liquid. Combine ½ cup reserved liquid with grapefruit juice and sugar in saucepan. Bring to a boil. Stir in pectin (Certo). Return to a boil; boil hard for one full minute. Skim off foam with a spoon.

Quickly pour into hot sterilized jelly jars, leaving ¼-inch headspace; cover at once with metal lids and screw on bands. Process in boiling-water bath 10 minutes. Yield: 4 half pints.

Suitable herbs to substitute for savory are sweet marjoram and oregano. Change the fruit juice to lemon juice or an orange-lemon juice mixture. If using fresh herbs instead of dried, use twice the amount.

Serve jellies with cream cheese and crackers or use as a vegetable or meat glaze. Savory Jelly can be served with green beans, and Marjoram Jelly, with baked chicken.

the seasons they aren't cultivating their five acres of plants.

"In the spring, our shows are plant-related," Marlene says. "Then we close for the summer and grow everything."

Beginning the first Saturday in November, Barbara and Marlene maintain a stall at the Carroll County Farmers Market in Westminster, Maryland. "We're there every Saturday for seven weeks, and people have come to look for us. They know we have things like orris root or oils for potpourris. Each week we take some crafts, and they never know what they'll find in addition to the standard things."

On weekends, their log cabin is open to the public. And then there's the holiday open house. Visitors sample freshly baked treats and sip spiced tea as they browse among tabletop herb trees, corn husk figures, and jars of herb jelly. (Marlene's herb jelly recipe is on the preceding page. Instructions for Barbara's corn husk Santa are on page 40.)

Barbara describes what makes their business unusual: "A lot of people who work with dried flowers buy them from somebody else. We create our products start to finish."

"So many herb shops buy and resell," Marlene adds. "Eighty to 90 percent of the things we sell are the things we have grown." As for the rest, Marlene says, "We're just lucky to be in an area that's rich in craftspeople."

"A lot of them are members of the Pennsylvania Guild of Craftsmen, which is a juried group," Barbara explains. "They're quilters, weavers. And these people are our friends. When I buy a handcrafted item, I

Right: In the den of the Steele home, Barbara combines quilts and coverlets, wooden and metal figures, jugs and other pieces she's collected to create a stunning effect. All she needs to do to decorate for the season is arrange a grouping of Santas and hang garlands and bunches of dried flowers.

Left: This small log cabin, a stone's throw from Barbara Steele's 19th-century home, is where the two women welcome customers and show off their wares. During the holiday season, they hold an open house, and visitors are treated to a sampling of their products and to the crafts of their friends, which are also for sale.

---

like to get an idea of the person who made it. I don't just buy something to fit a decorating scheme." Then she laughs, "Therefore I have a very jumbled scheme."

It may be jumbled by some standards, but it lends itself well to holiday decorating, as the pictures on these pages show. Before the log cabin, Barbara opened the doors of her 19th-century home for the holiday open house. Now she and Marlene invite their friends to exhibit their crafts alongside the sweetly scented trees, wreaths, and baskets at Alloway Gardens and Herb Farm's holiday open house.

Above: During the holiday open house, herbs and flowers in many incarnations are arrayed in the main room of the log cabin shop at Alloway Gardens and Herb Farm.

Opposite: Upstairs in Alloway's log cabin, an antique bed covered with a quilt sets the mood for the items displayed there. In the spring and summer, Barbara and Marlene nurture flowers and herbs, and in the winter, they use the ones they've dried to make gorgeous decorations like those shown here.

11

Angelic Corn Husk Dolls

At the moment, Jocelyn Mostrom is explaining why the Edwardian period is her favorite right now. "The dolls from that period were so wonderful—no expense was spared on their making." And Jocelyn knows her dolls.

She is a corn husk artist, who pulls forms from corn husks as no other can. And for Christmas, Jocelyn is busy decorating her home and tree with the fruits of her talent—delicate creatures that seem to rise out of a cloud of flowing husks. Each angel wears a halo and holds a small garland of dried flowers; figures of women and children hold bouquets of dried flowers. "I have made dolls out of every possible medium," explains Jocelyn. "And the subtle draping achieved with the corn husk is quite lovely." Bunches of baby's breath and dried-flower garlands sprinkled with lacy ribbons make a splendid accompaniment for her Edwardian-style dolls.

The base, the head, and the hands of the dolls are porcelain that has been tinted by Jocelyn, and the husks are dyed to gentle pastel shades. All the flowers used in her garlands and wreaths are grown in her backyard garden, and dozens of bunches of flowers hang from the beams in the kitchen of her Maryland home.

Jocelyn is a self-taught corn husk artist and has spent 14 years perfecting her technique. The suppleness of the corn husk allows a motion in the dolls' clothing that is Jocelyn's pride as well as her trademark.

Opposite: A shower of corn husk beauties covers the branches of Jocelyn Mostrom's Edwardian-style Christmas tree. "It's been fun pulling corn husk dolls out of the folksy art form to make it a more refined art," she says. Several lengths of dried-flower garlands wrap around the tree to form a continuous flower chain. To make your own dried-flower garland, start with a rope base (width depends on tree size). Use a hot-glue gun to attach the dried flowers to the garland. For better coverage, group several blooms together and glue in bunches. Fill in any holes with additional flowers.

Above: A vision of ethereal splendor is created from the quite ordinary corn husk. The angel's face and arms are porcelain that Jocelyn has tinted. A wisp-of-gold halo crowns this angel, and she holds a garland composed of one corn husk flower and several dried flowers. Lace sleeves and trim supply additional richness to the softly muted colors.

13

She shares this expertise through classes taught in her studio and at the Smithsonian Institution. The six-hour session includes making a corn husk wreath, doll, or angel. Jocelyn doesn't believe in teaching with many rules. "If you get the effect you want, that's wonderful, that's right," she explains.

And don't expect to find any sketches for future dolls. Jocelyn says she just starts. "The designs in my head are in motion, and I have to catch them. My design evolves, rather than being constructed."

With her husband to help seed the garden and her sons to help with the gathering, Jocelyn is able to capture many of those images and transform them into elegant corn husk designs.

Above: Corn husk bows and flowers are also specialties of the house. Here they are combined with lace and dried flowers to make a corn husk wreath. Jocelyn dyes some of the corn husk pieces. Others she leaves natural. Most of the flowers are used in their naturally dried colors. Gracing the center of the fluffy wreath is one of Jocelyn's porcelain-and-corn husk ladies.

Left: Surrounded by the tools of her trade, Jocelyn fluffs a corn husk wreath with the handle of a paintbrush. All the flowers used in her creations are grown and dried at Jocelyn's home. During the fall she teaches classes in her studio and sometimes conducts them at the Smithsonian Institution.

A Starr Collection

Atlanta artist Susan Starr is the first to tell you that she is a weaver, not a paper-maker. But allow your eyes to focus on her Christmas tree and your head will swim. Gliding across the branches are delicate pastel paper fish constructed from hand-made paper. "I lived in Europe growing up, and we always had fish on the tree," says Susan. "They were good luck."

A weaver by profession, Susan is an art-ist in her heart and is always experiment-ing with textiles. She has also been making paper for the past three years. The slow, exacting process of grinding the base ma-terial to a pulp and adding chemicals and dye produces soft, interestingly textured, one-of-a-kind sheets of paper.

Often, Susan will weave yarns left over from some of her tapestries into the paper to add extra sparkle. Then, she sculpts the paper into a whimsical fish, a tiny, plump gift box, a folded fan held together by gold ribbon, or she may layer sheets, one upon the other, to form a paper wreath.

Above: A pastel paper fan flutters open and hangs from a satin ribbon, and tiny sculpted-paper orna-ments, plump with surprises, dot the branches. Floating in an ocean of evergreen and baby's breath is a glittering example of the artist's paper fish.

Right: Susan Starr ties the final touches to her handmade-paper fans. "Papermaking is an out-growth of my weaving," she explains. "Usually I cut up fabric and weave it together. Now, I'm pressing it back together." Attending workshops in Boston and California convinced Susan that papermaking was worth her attention. Last year she decided to have a Christmas show of her ornaments, wreaths, and garlands, and sold more than she had ever ima-gined she would sell. Susan also made several wreaths to benefit Atlanta's Children's Hospital.

Above: Sunlight dances across the glittering surface of Susan Starr's paper-adorned Christmas tree. "I really like pastel colors. And it's still easy to create something festive without using red and green," says Susan.

An Oklahoma Holiday: City Meets Country

It's the best of both worlds. Nancy and Joe Proctor live in the middle of a 140-acre farm in rural Oklahoma. They operate a business called The American Folk Art Company, designing and producing furniture and decorative objects. But promoting this business takes these sophisticated country dwellers to some of the most exciting cities in the country.

They have showrooms in San Francisco, Palm Beach, Santa Fe, Dallas, and High Point (the prestigious furniture center in North Carolina). In addition, they travel throughout America and abroad, keeping a finger on the international design pulse.

Right: The great room in the Proctors' Oklahoma country home is dressed for the season in a style suited to the owners and their business. Near the windows is a horn chandelier from England. Beneath it are samples of their furniture and decorative pieces, including a small "salesmen's sample" willow chair. Horns are a theme that they use extensively, especially on the mantel, where the horn has been hollowed out to hold candles.

Below: A copse of persimmon trees rises in front of the barn Nancy and her father built. Among the trees stands a herd of sycamore reindeer, ears pricked as though alert to the coyotes and raccoons that also call the Proctors' 140 acres home.

18

Above: Dramatic animal-print pillows create a so-phisticated effect when paired with the dyed willow chair made by the Proctors' American Folk Art Com-pany. The grapevine tree and wooden rabbits around it are also made by the company. Hand-carved wooden dogs, a wooden bead garland, tiny white lights, and small brass hunting horns complete the festive decorations on the tree.

Left: Nancy and Joe Proctor enjoy the comforts of their beautiful home, built in the countryside of Oklahoma about an hour's drive north of Tulsa. For the holidays, they enjoy grapevine trees, some deco-rated simply with white lights. In the background is an arrangement of pinecones and berries made dis-tinctive with the addition of horn, which is used throughout their holiday decorations.

It's an amazing mix, and one that is reflected in their home and in their Christmas celebrations. Nancy and Joe fill their house with the stylish folk art furniture that has become their company's trademark. In the great room, they have a grouping of willow chairs dyed a rich black-brown, a cedar chair with a flowing bow carved into its back, carved wooden animals, and a tabletop grapevine tree decorated for the holidays with a collection of hand-carved wooden dogs.

The dog ornaments were a gift. "Every year we have a different tree," Nancy says. "This year we filled the grapevine tree with dogs. We're partial to dogs. We have nine, with names like Chutney, Dudley, Lucy, and Blossom.

"Our decorations are not commercial. We use strung wooden beads and other country kinds of things." Some of the Proctors' decorations are presents from the neighbors. "At Christmas we go around taking them presents. They give us wonderful things, canned goods like jellies and pickles, and things they've made from heirloom quilts. One friend gave us place mats, made from a quilt, with the most delicate pockets for holding napkins."

The Proctors have a guest house, which they decorate for Christmas, making it ready for the family members who visit during the holidays. "We have a big school bell on the porch that we ring to call them up to the house for meals."

They are living the idyllic country life, dreamed about by so many in big cities. The Proctors know the dreams only too well. Nancy lived in Tulsa before moving to the farm 20 years ago. Joe spent 18 years running executive conferences for the Harvard Business School Program, among others. He was based in San Francisco and New York, with residences in both places, and his work took him all over the world. One day his destination was Oklahoma. He met Nancy, they fell in love, and they were married. He asked her to join him in his twin-coast life-style.

"She said, why don't you try it out here? and I thought, what am I going to do?" Joe explains. He started experimenting with willow chairs, and he and Nancy took the chairs to showrooms in Dallas, where they were a tremendous success. "We had more orders than we knew how to fill, and we came back and started working with local craftspeople." The Proctors hired staff, expanded their exposure, and The American Folk Art Company was off and running.

The dream of so many harried urban dwellers is the reality of life for Nancy and Joe Proctor: living and working in the beautiful Oklahoma countryside, while maintaining ties with vital cities across the nation. It gives them full exposure to and an appreciation of both kinds of life-styles. And it blends beautifully into their country holiday celebrations in rural Oklahoma.

Above: In the center of the Proctors' dining table, an English silver mug with a horn handle holds a simple arrangement of tulips and carnations. The holiday season is evoked very subtly with bits of ribbon and greenery, a few berries, and a small package, topped with natural materials, that rests among the fruit surrounding the mug.

21

Designs from Creation

Margaret Furlong wanted everything right for the first Christmas in her new studio. The success of her business had warranted a most welcomed move. And Margaret decided to celebrate by decorating the space to its renovated rafters.

Her plan was two-fold: "I wanted to share ideas on how to decorate for Christmas using my porcelain pieces," Margaret explained. "And to create for the people who work here and those who come here a beautiful and festive environment for the celebration of Christ's birthday."

It is this unceasing attention to detail and balance that allows Margaret Furlong to transform memories, impressions, and personal experiences into delicate bisque porcelain hearts, angels, and stars.

Margaret and her husband, Jerry Alexander, work together in the business. Jerry handles sales and distribution to leave Margaret time to design. "I always have plenty of ideas, so the task is in making them work."

The acclaim she has received for her pristine bisque porcelain figures is proof that her designs "work." Her figures have adorned trees at the White House and the Oregon state capitol. Margaret began experimenting with the shell motif several years ago at the request of a friend. She has expanded on this early concept because she sees her shell designs as "a celebration of God's beautiful nature—a design from creation."

This spiritual outlook translates to all of the Furlong designs. Last year's limited-edition angel carried an image of the sun

---

Opposite: With several dolls borrowed from her daughter, Margaret creates "a child's vision of Christmas" in an antique armoire. On either door, shell wreaths are encircled with greenery, and the trees are sprinkled with designs known as "A Pocketful of Stars," "Oh, Sweetest Heart," and "Catch a Falling Star." Porcelain pins are lined up in their Furlong-designed packaging.

Above: Carriage House Studio in Salem, Oregon, is home to Margaret Furlong's well-known bisque porcelain designs. The renovation of an old brick warehouse provided the business with the wide-open spaces of a contemporary studio and showroom— and just in time to decorate for Christmas. The front door wears a wreath adorned with shell stars.

Above: Margaret Furlong, daughter Caitlin, and husband, Jerry Alexander, pose in front of one of the angels that is part of the limited edition known as "Gifts from God." Each family member has a role in the successful business: Margaret is the designer, Jerry is business manager, and Caitlin supplies inspiration. "It's great having a team," says Margaret. "We work very well together."

Above: Stars and angels, showcased in a pine armoire, display Margaret's designs and decorating ideas. Margaret calls this her "Oregon vignette." Noble firs and shasta trees, both native to Oregon, provide the greenery, and small stars are attached to limes by pins. Margaret uses the limes to represent the bountiful northwest and the pineapple to symbolize hospitality.

24

as a symbol of light and enlightenment; this year's angel holds stars as a symbol of eternity, and in memory of her father. The idea behind the porcelain heart series known as "A Handful of Hearts" is "to sprinkle your life with images of love." And the bouquets her smaller angels carry are tied with bows inspired by the charm of her daughter's girlhood. A new line for 1988 is "Stars by the Yard," which is a yard of 1½" porcelain stars on a double strand of ribbon.

All designs begin in Margaret's mind and quickly make their way to three-dimensional shapes. After she makes a model, it is cast in a material to make a master mold. Margaret makes a master mold for every design and tailors the production to an efficient and pleasant process. Last she writes up the procedure, complete with quality standards. Only then does the design leave her hands.

To achieve the snow-white appearance that is her trademark, Margaret uses an imported grolleg, which contains a very pure, yet pliable clay. Most of the parts of the figures are made by press molding, but several different processes work together to complete a piece. "Everyone is always so impressed when they see that all the designs are handmade," she says. Even more impressive are the thought, skill, and time invested in each design.

Above: Porcelain "Oh, Sweetest Hearts" mingle with fabric hearts on a small Noble fir tree. Topping the tree is a porcelain shell wreath. All ornaments have small holes at the top so that ribbon or wire may be threaded through as hangers.

Left: Margaret's skilled hands add final touches to what will become a master mold for her shell star designs. Her designs are made from the purest form of clay offering pliability and a very white surface. This quality, plus the intricate detailing, makes Furlong designs works of art.

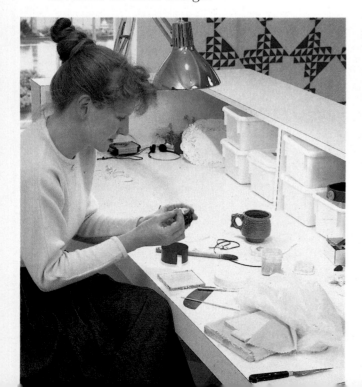

25

In a Studio by the Sea

Sea breezes ease the warmth of the October sun on Florida's panhandle. Christmas seems more than just a couple of months away as people wearing short-sleeved cottons gather for a decorative-painting workshop. But step inside Priscilla Hauser's Studio by the Sea, and the balmy weather outside gives way to the sights, sounds, and smells of the holiday season.

Rows of tables are covered with white paper. At each place, Priscilla and her assistants have painted the names of workshop participants and affixed little wreaths. One member of Priscilla's team, Genie Amberson, brought her church's Christmas tree to the shop and spent over 100 hours wiring tiny white lights to it. It's decorated with paintbrushes, palettes, and little whisks from one of Priscilla's creations.

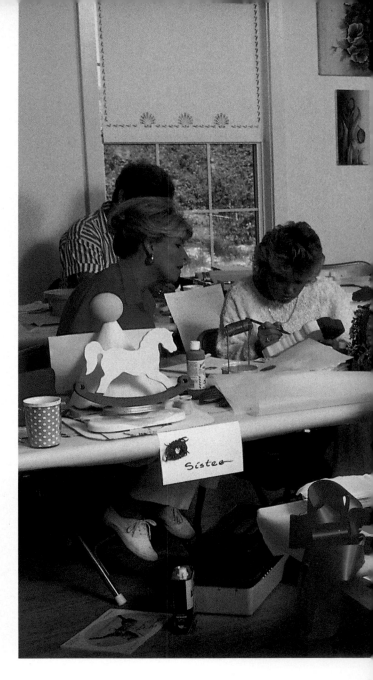

Above: Priscilla Hauser's Studio by the Sea, on Florida's panhandle, is a short drive from Destin on one side and Panama City on the other. The charming location offers the pleasure of a sunny beach—if students can put down their brushes long enough to explore it. Priscilla and her husband, Jerry, decided to open the studio a few years ago, with the long-range goal of dividing their time between the seaside and their home in Tulsa.

As the participants arrive on a Sunday afternoon, their greetings and laughter drown out the recorded carols that will accompany their efforts over the next week. A cupboard is filled with the items they'll be making: a large wooden Santa, teddy bear and rocking horse toys, an angel, a Christmas basket filled with painted eggs, and a dimensional glass wall hanging that's a painted wreath in a gold leaf frame. All of the raw materials are attractively arranged and waiting for the students. Priscilla will guide them through the steps, easing any anxieties they might have with her enthusiasm and encouragement.

26

Above: Even though Priscilla doesn't begin classes until 9 a.m., the doors to the Studio by the Sea open at 7:30, so that eager students can get an early start. Many stay until seven or later in the evening, putting into practice the techniques they've learned during the day.

Left: Priscilla can be rambunctious and she can be funny, but when she demonstrates painting techniques, she exhibits a professionalism that explains her worldwide acclaim. In 1984 she represented the U.S. in the Netherlands as part of an international team of artists gathered to produce work to benefit the Worldwide Wildlife Federation. In 1972, her efforts led to the formation of the National Society of Tole and Decorative Painters; today the organization has over 30,000 members.

"The thing that has been most important to me over the years is showing people how to paint and that it doesn't take talent," Priscilla said. "It doesn't take any more talent to paint than it does to cook, to sew. It's wonderful to have God-given talent, but anyone can learn to paint.

"I teach using patterns. Musicians work from scores. When you are learning to cook, you cook from a recipe. Musical scores are patterns; recipes are patterns. We have to have different consistencies for paint the same way oven temperatures have to be right."

Priscilla has proven that her technique works. She has published extensively. She has had, and continues to have, programs on the Public Broadcasting System. And she conducts workshops in Florida and in her hometown of Tulsa, Oklahoma.

She not only has students in every corner of this country, but also in Portugal, the Azores, Japan, Germany, England, Africa, and the Netherlands. They find their lives made richer by the skills she's taught them. Some students have craft shops, some use her techniques to teach classes, most exhibit and sell their work at craft shows and in shops. And even when they've had hundreds of hours of instruction, many come back to be re-energized and inspired by Priscilla.

She leans over them, one by one, as they put paint-filled brushes to paper, and she says, "Press down, that's right. Now pull! Pull! Lift up! See? That's a beautiful stroke!" And they smile back at her, enjoying each success as if it were the first.

Above: Genie Amberson and Sistee Knight (shown here) and Jane Jenkins (not shown) go to great lengths to provide tasty, nutritious meals for workshop participants during the week-long sessions. Here, Jane and Genie have prepared box lunches with a twist—the boxes are imaginatively wrapped Christmas presents.

Left: In Priscilla Hauser's Studio by the Sea, a fire in the stove helps provide atmosphere for the Christmas classes she conducts. Surrounding the stove are objects she's made and collected over the years. Prominently featured in a large wreath is a special favorite of Priscilla's—an angel candle holder by the artist Peter Hunt. Hunt worked in the first half of the century and is considered one of America's foremost decorative painters.

WELCOME THE SEASON

That jolly gent who is the inspiration for countless tales and traditions will be warming up the sleigh soon. Before he alights on your rooftop, make sure everything is ready. On the following pages, gorgeous decorations for everywhere—from tabletops to front yards—await your choice. You'll find more than a few things to turn St. Nick's head this year.

Folk-Art Santas Make Fantasy Tabletops

It seems that everyone has his own image of Santa—from the length of his beard to the girth of his belly. Imbued with charisma by the hands of loving artists, rustic St. Nicks will lend Christmas cheer wherever you put them. Start your own collection this season; then add more every year. Look for them on your travels—you'll encounter a variety of lovable characters.

On the preceding pages, Santas sally forth against a wintry backdrop, a primitive painting framed in burled wood. There's a crackled St. Nick, a wedge-headed Santa with package aloft, a diminutive elf—as much beard as body—with switches in hand, and a pottery Santa. One old gent's

bag has tiny books and carved toys. And a chiseled midnight cowboy cheers on the reindeer who pulls his chariot.

Opposite, Santas sport individual personalities, particularly a stilt-legged, pipe-smoking, wreath-balancing fellow. In a holly tree berried with sweet-smelling rose-hips, carved wooden cardinals jauntily perch amid miniature birdhouses and basket birds' nests.

Below, a gracefully crafted Santa holding a tiny gift is surrounded by folk art—tin candlesticks, wooden evergreens, an antique mold chalkware lamb, a German feather tree, and a framed bit of an 1842 Pennsylvania coverlet.

Cross-Stitch Sampler With a Special Verse

"And the light was for all time and the love was for all men." This touching verse is cross-stitched in a traditional sampler, complete with an alphabet and rows of hearts and flowers. Include the year the stitchery was done and your name, and this meaningful work becomes a family heirloom, a cherished Christmas tradition.

Materials:
charts begin on page 128
9″ x 11″ piece of 18-count white Aida cloth
embroidery floss (see color key)
#24 tapestry needle
wooden tray with 7″ x 10″ window for design

Following chart and color key, stitch design with 1 strand of floss. Place finished sampler in wooden tray.

34

Simply Elegant Greetings

Lovely enough to be framed, these simply elegant poinsettia greeting cards will delight their recipients this Christmas and are sure to be treasured and displayed for Christmases to come. The distinctive blossoms and leaves of the cheery poinsettia are cut from brightly colored paper and Christmas gift wrap and are then artfully arranged on a contrasting background. Try your own color combinations to achieve dramatic or subtle effects.

For each card, you will need a 7″ x 10″ piece of paper folded in half or a 5″ x 7″ notecard, colored and metallic paper or gift wrap, and a glue stick.

For patterns, refer to page 128. Cut out patterns from colored paper. Cut a 4″-square piece of colored paper; center it on card and glue in place. Referring to the photograph, arrange the elements on the card. Glue them in place.

Beaded Baubles

Beads in jewel tones of garnet, emerald, and gold are embroidered onto Aida cloth and perforated paper to form a sophisticated gift bag and dazzling ornaments.

The large ornament is made by working the design on two separate pieces of perforated paper and then stitching both pieces together. Even purchased ornaments can easily be enhanced with variations on the pattern worked on perforated paper.

Materials:
patterns, charts begin on page 128
2 (3½″-square) pieces of perforated paper (large ornament)
2 (2″-square) pieces of perforated paper (ball ornament)
6″ x 13″ piece of 14-count Aida (bag)
garnet, emerald, and gold colored glass beads (2 tubes each for large ornament, 1 tube each for bag and ball ornament)
#10 crewel needle
#24 tapestry needle (bag)
craft knife
masking tape
craft glue
20″ piece of metallic cord (bag)
15″ piece (¼″-wide) green ribbon (ball ornament)
metallic cord (ball ornament)

TIPS FOR BEAD STITCHING: Divide beads by color and pour into shallow containers. Thread needle and bring up through paper or fabric at beginning of first stitch, leaving a tail of at least 1″ to catch under the first several stitches. Referring to chart and color key for each project, attach beads individually with half-cross stitches. Beginning at top of design, work horizontal rows. All half crosses must slant in the same direction but can be worked from left to right or from right to left. Bring needle up, pick up bead with tip, and take needle down. To begin and end a thread, or to move from one area to another, weave thread securely through stitching on back. If any beads appear to be loose, stitch through them again.

Note: When stitching on paper, avoid tearing by bringing the needle straight up and down through holes in 2 motions.

For each design, find center of cloth or paper and mark on back. Count from center to find starting point. For gift bag, bind fabric edges with masking tape. Work all designs according to charts. For large ornament, work design twice, leaving 2 rows unstitched on all sides. For gift bag, include corner motifs on graph and leave a ¾″ margin at bottom. For ball ornament, stitch design twice.

FINISHING: For large ornament, after completing design, trim away excess paper, cutting through the row of holes outside stitching area. Align both worked pieces, wrong sides facing, and join them by working a running stitch through the previously worked outer row of holes around both pieces. To make beaded loop, bring needle up through hole at top point; string beads, put needle back through same hole, and continue with running stitch. Add strung beads at outer edges and center points by threading beads on needle and continuing with running stitch.

For gift bag, remove masking tape, place stitchery face down on a towel, and press with warm iron. Fold in half, right sides facing, and stitch sides together with a ½″ seam allowance. Stitch a ½″ hem on raw edge. Turn bag and press from back. Thread tapestry needle with metallic cord and stitch 1″ from top for drawstring.

For ball ornament, cut out stitched designs, leaving small border on all sides. For outline beading, thread needle, and beginning at one back corner, string 3 to 6 beads at a time around design, with a series of backstitches around outer edge of design. Add or subtract beads as needed on corners and curves. Apply glue to back of designs and attach to opposite sides of ball. Glue metallic braid around center of ball. Tie green ribbon at top.

A Basket of Christmas Tulips

This cheery pieced, quilted, and stenciled basket makes a unique holiday door decoration. However, the design and colors are suitable year-round.

Materials:
patterns begin on page 128
1 yard dark green pindot
3″ x 12″ piece of solid cream fabric
4″ x 12″ piece of red pindot
16″ x 28″ piece of thin batting
matching thread
red quilting thread
mylar or stencil paper
craft knife
stencil paints (red, green)
stencil brush
¾ yard (⅞″-wide) cream ribbon

Note: Use ¼″ seam allowance. Seams should be pressed in the direction of the darkest fabric whenever possible. If you do not want to stencil the tulip blocks on the basket, you can appliqué the pattern instead, using scraps of red and green pindot fabrics. To appliqué, add ⅛″ seam allowance to tulip patterns.

From green pindot, cut 10 triangles (B). From cream fabric, cut 4 diamonds (C). Following stenciling directions, stencil tulips in the centers of the 4 cream diamonds. Stitch triangles and diamonds together as shown in Diagram 1. From red pindot, cut 2 (1½″ x 12″) strips. With right sides facing, sew one 12″ edge of a strip to top edge of pieced block. Stitch other strip to bottom edge. (See Diagram 2.)

From green pindot, cut a 10″ x 12″ rectangle. With right sides facing, stitch a 12″ edge of rectangle to bottom edge of red strip. Transfer basket pattern (D) to paper, and pin paper pattern to the pieced unit, matching top edges and centers. Cut fabric to match pattern.

From green pindot, cut 3 from pattern (D) for the basket back and lining. From batting, cut 2 from pattern (D). Set aside.

To make handles, from green pindot, cut 6 (1½″ x 22″) strips (3 for each handle). Place each strip right side down, turn long edges ¼″ to wrong side, and press. Fold strip in half, wrong sides together. Machine-stitch 3 strips together at one end to secure. Beginning at stitched end, braid the 3 strips together. Repeat for other handle. Handles should measure 15″. Trim unstitched end if necessary, and machine-stitch across braid at that point to secure ends.

Lay basket front right side up. With raw edges aligned, pin the ends of a braided handle to basket top, 3″ from sides. Baste in place. Repeat for basket back.

Baste batting pieces to wrong sides of basket front and back. With right sides facing, lay one lining piece on pieced basket front and the other lining piece on the basket back; pin.

Stitch front and lining piece together; then stitch back and remaining lining piece together, leaving open as indicated on pattern. (Be careful not to catch handles in seam.) Trim corners of both pieces, clip at angles, and turn. Slipstitch openings closed. (You now have 2 sewn-together basket pieces.)

Using red thread, quilt around each stenciled tulip and quilt-in-the-ditch around each cream diamond. Machine-quilt the diamond design on green pindot basket front as indicated on pattern piece (D). Machine-quilt back in same manner.

With wrong sides facing, place basket front on basket back. Starting at center of bottom edge, slipstitch front and back together across bottom and around side. Repeat for other side.

Tie a bow with cream ribbon and attach to bottom red strip.

STENCIL DIRECTIONS

From mylar or stencil paper, cut out the stencils for the tulip in 3 separate parts as indicated. Be sure to use a sharp craft knife. Stencil a tulip (as illustrated on the pattern) in the center of a cream diamond, using red for the flower and green for the leaves.

Diagram 1—Stitching Triangles (B) to Diamonds (C)

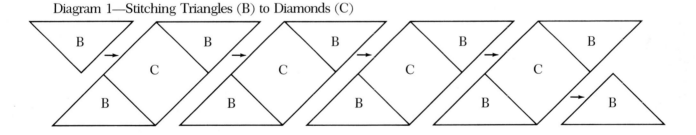

Diagram 2—Stitching 1½″ x 12″ Strips to Pieced Block

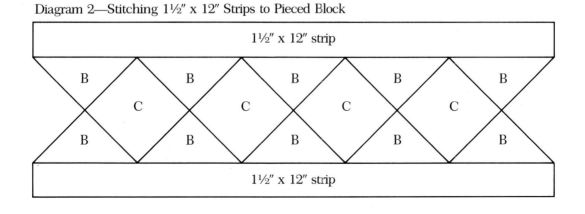

Corn Husk Santa

Made from country craft staples, this Santa is a vision of texture. The old gent's flowing robes are made from dyed corn husks and trimmed in natural wool, which also shapes his bodacious beard.

Materials:
25 to 30 (approximately 6″ x 9″) corn husks (or substitute tamale wrappers, available in specialty food stores)
large bucket
bleach
scarlet (or other dark red) fabric dye
distilled white vinegar
towels
cotton balls
heavy thread
white pipe cleaner
21″ (¼″) brown jute cord
hot-glue gun and glue sticks
natural white wool ends
small purchased basket
small purchased tree
4 (3″- to 5″-long) twigs
20″ twine
clear matte spray sealer
fine-tip permanent black marker

Soak corn husks in warm water until pliable, about 10-15 minutes. (To remove mildew and lighten husks, add bleach to the water.) Rinse husks with clean water. For head, body, and arms, set aside 6 husks.

To dye husks, add 1 package of red dye to 1½ quarts of water. Place remaining dampened husks in simmering dye bath. Leave husks in dye until they turn dark red. (Husks will dry a lighter color.) Rinse husks in cool water, adding a little vinegar to set the color. Place husks on towels to absorb excess water. Corn husks can be shaped only while they are damp and flexible, so try to use husks within 24 hours. To avoid mildew, store damp husks in a cool place, sealed in a plastic bag.

For the head and body, use undyed husks. Select a smooth, wide husk to cover face. With rough side of husk up, place 2 cotton balls in the center. Fold lengthwise edges of husk, covering cotton balls. Twist corn husk 3 times at each end of cotton balls, leaving an excess of 3½″ at both ends. Pull one end down to other end and tie together to form the head and neck. (See Diagram 1.) Set aside.

For arms, tear a piece of damp husk 2″-wide and longer than the pipe cleaner. Lay pipe cleaner lengthwise on husk; roll up in husk. Fold husk ends that extend beyond pipe cleaner toward center of pipe cleaner and tie 1″ from each end. To make sleeves, wrap a 5″-long dyed husk loosely around pipe cleaner arm piece and tie in the center. Trim sleeves to expose hands.

To form upper body, place arm piece under head, between husk pieces covering head. To form chest, insert 2 cotton balls between husk pieces below arm piece. Tie securely at waist with thread.

For skirt, use 9-12 dyed husks of equal length. Placing the narrow ends of husks at the waist with the wide ends curving up around doll's head, overlap husks to create a full skirt. (See Diagram 2.) Securely tie

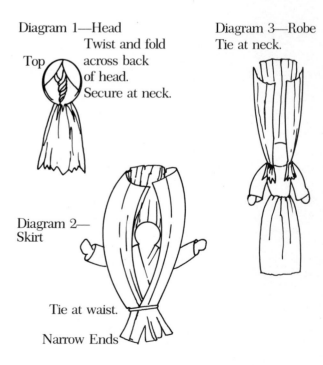

Diagram 1—Head
Twist and fold across back of head. Secure at neck.
Top

Diagram 3—Robe
Tie at neck.

Diagram 2—Skirt

Tie at waist.

Narrow Ends

husks at waist; then pull husks down to form skirt. Tie a length of thread around fullness of skirt to hold shape while drying. Trim bottom of skirt to correct proportion and stand doll upright.

For robe, use 3 dyed husks (1 wide husk for the back of the head and 2 husks for the sides of the head). Arrange husks (rough sides toward head) with narrow ends pointed down and wide ends curving up around doll's head. (See Diagram 3.) Tie husks around neck with thread. Bend husks down over body. Tie brown cord around waist, and trim husks at bottom of doll. Bend arms at elbows. Let doll dry completely before assembly.

For hair and robe trim, use glue gun to apply small dots of glue to head and around face area. Twist lengths of wool, and press into glue dots. For hat, cut a 3″ circle from 1 dyed husk and shape into a cone. Glue hat on head. Twist a length of wool and glue around bottom edge of hat.

Glue small tree into basket. Tie basket to doll arm with twine. Tie a small bundle of twigs together, add a touch of glue, and tie with twine. Through the hand loop, glue twigs to hand. Spray the doll with sealer to preserve color and wool. Draw eyes with fine-tip marker.

Tapestry Flower Ornaments

Like exquisitely detailed needlepoint pillows, these richly hued, tapestry flower ornaments add elegance to any room they grace. Their jewellike presence belying the simplicity of their design, they are made of perforated paper and embroidered, using cross-stitch techniques. Edged with gold, these tapestry-inspired prisms are delicate holiday accents and become lovely year-round sachets when filled with fragrant potpourri.

Materials (each ornament):
patterns, charts begin on page 128
9″ x 12″ perforated paper in desired color
Note: **If colored paper is unavailable, white perforated paper can be *lightly* sprayed with acrylic paint.**
embroidery floss
#20 tapestry needle
craft knife
straightedge
craft glue in tube
silk pins
thread
1 yard gold cording

Transfer pattern to paper, being careful that Line AB lies directly on a horizontal row of perforations, and cut out. Using this hexagon as a template, place it over the paper, hold paper and template up to a light source, and line up the perforations before tracing and cutting out hexagons. Cut out 7 more hexagons.

On right sides of paper hexagons, lightly score along fold lines.

Following chart, use 3 strands of floss to work designs.

Separate the hexagons into 2 groups, each having 2 hexagons of each color variation. Begin assembling the top of the prism by arranging the 4 pieces as they will be in the finished piece, alternating flower colors. Fold triangular side tabs in and glue adjacent tabs together with a bead of glue. Let glue dry before gluing remaining tabs together. Repeat this procedure for the bottom half of the prism. Let glue dry.

Fold in remaining tabs of each prism half and glue them together, alternating the flower color of panels above and below. To secure while glue dries, gently insert

silk pins through perforations in both top and bottom sections and lace thread around pins. Remove pins and thread when glue is dry.

To make a hanger, fold gold cord 4″ from end and tie a slipknot 3″ from fold. Tuck short end of the cord into top of prism and position knot over it. Wrap the long end of cord vertically around edges of ornament, attaching along the seam with a thin line of glue. When cord has been wrapped completely around ornament, cut cord and tuck end into prism top, under loop. Wrap second vertical seam in same manner, omitting loop. Secure loop and cord ends with dot of glue. Glue cord around horizontal seam last, tucking end into a corner opening and securing with a dot of glue.

Decorate Your Lawn With Forest Friends

Decorate your lawn for the holidays with these bold and cheery forest friends. Made of plywood, they are brought to life with enamel paint and brightened with a crisp checkerboard pattern that becomes the cardinal's wing and the reindeer's collar of Christmas colors.

Materials:
patterns begin on page 128
2' x 4' piece of ⅜" plywood (reindeer)
8" x 9" piece of ⅜" plywood (cardinal)
1 (36"-long) 1 x 1 (for stakes)
jigsaw or hacksaw
electric drill with countersink and
  ⅛" bit
sandpaper
wood filler
craft glue
4 (1") #10 flat-head wood screws
enamel paint (white, red, green, and
  brown)
model paint (black)
flat-bristle paintbrushes in widths of
  2", ½", and ¼"
small paintbrush for details
15" (⅛"-wide) red ribbon or twine

Trace reindeer and cardinal patterns onto back of plywood and cut out shapes, sawing from back to front. Mark and drill hole in cardinal shape, following pattern.

Cut wood for stakes into two 18" lengths, cutting one end of each into a wedge. On back of reindeer, position stakes vertically and in centers of legs, allowing stakes to extend 6" below bottom of legs. Trace around stakes on legs. Remove stakes and apply glue within traced areas. Glue stakes in place; let dry. To secure, countersink holes through center front of one leg and one stake, measuring from edges to determine center. Attach stake to leg with wood screws. Repeat for second leg.

With wood filler, fill in screw holes and imperfections in plywood; sand to smooth fronts and edges.

Set shapes on wood scraps and paint backs and edges. Paint reindeer brown and cardinal red. When dry, turn over and paint fronts. Let dry.

Transfer details to fronts of shapes and paint, following patterns and photograph. Let dry overnight. To place reindeer on lawn, make pilot holes in the ground for stakes; then, tapping the tops of the stakes alternately, drive them into holes. To hang cardinal from branch, lace ribbon or twine through hole in cardinal and tie to branch.

Knit St. Nick
In the Nick of Time

Knitting gives old St. Nick a new look. In this clever design, large areas are knitted; then a few details are embroidered. Use this quaint character as a mantel decoration or in a wreath. Or, because he's soft and safe to hug—give him to a child for a Christmas toy.

Materials:
charts begin on page 128
knitting worsted: 2 ounces red; 1 ounce each white, green; 3 yards each pink, black; scrap of blue
size 7 knitting needles (or size to obtain gauge)
size 7 double-pointed knitting needles
tapestry needle
stuffing
size G crochet hook

GAUGE: 9 sts and 14 rows = 2″
FINISHED SIZE: approximately 10″ high
FRONT: With white and single-pointed needles, cast on 23 sts. K in St st following chart for front, changing colors and dec or inc as indicated. *Note:* To avoid holes, twist old over new when changing colors.

BACK: With white and single-pointed needles, cast on 23 sts. Follow the chart for the back, changing colors and dec or inc as indicated.

BOTTOM: With red, cast on 7 sts. Follow chart for bottom, changing colors and inc or dec as indicated.

FINISHING: To add details to face and front: With blue, embroider French knots for eyes. With red, embroider a small straight stitch for mouth. With green, embroider cross-stitches down center front.

With right sides facing and leaving bottom open, sew front and back tog. Turn. Stuff firmly. Slipstitch bottom piece to doll.

BAG: With green and double-pointed needles, cast on 36 sts. Slip a marker on the needle after the last st to indicate the end of a round. [P 1 round, K 1 round] twice. Yo, k 2 tog around. K even in rounds until piece measures 4″ from beg.

Decrease rounds: Round 1: K 4, k 2 tog around. *Round 2:* K. *Round 3:* K 3, k 2 tog around. *Round 4:* K. *Round 5:* K 2, k 2 tog around. *Round 6:* K 1, k 2 tog around. *Round 7:* K 2 tog around. Cut yarn and thread end through rem sts. Pull tightly to gather.

With green and crochet hook, make a chain about 18″ long. Thread chain through the openings on bag. Tack the ends of the chain together.

Standard Knitting Abbreviations
st(s)—stitch(es)
St st—stockinette stitch (k 1 row, p 1 row)
k—knit
p—purl
dec—decrease
inc—increase
tog—together
yo—yarn over
beg—beginning
rem—remaining

Lambs Parade on a Patchwork Stocking

Classic quilting shapes in colorful calicos surround a stitchery inset, as patchwork and cross-stitch work together to make this country stocking. Cross-stitched lambs line up in a row and meander amidst flowers with a striking resemblance to hearts. A single larger heart flower is appliquéd on the stocking. This repeat of the motif, plus color coordination of fabric and floss, ties the mediums together.

Cross-stitch strip stitched on off-white Jo-belan 28 over 2 threads or Aida 14. The finished design size is 3″ x 6½″.

Materials:
completed cross-stitch; for chart with instructions, see patterns beginning on page 128
¾ yard of dark red miniprint
scraps of 100% cotton print (off-white, tan, and dark green)
49″ of matching green print piping
⅝ yard (⅛″-wide) dark red grosgrain ribbon
12″ x 18″ piece of batting

Note: All seam allowances are ¼″.
Transfer stocking bottom pattern to dark red fabric and cut 1. Extend stocking bottom pattern 7″; cut 3 full-size pieces (2 for lining and 1 for stocking back) from dark red miniprint. Cut 1 full-size stocking from batting. Trace and transfer remaining pattern pieces (except heart and leaf patterns) to fabrics indicated and cut out.

Referring to Diagram 1, construct sections 1 and 3. With right sides facing, sew all A, B, and C pieces together. Stitch sections 1, 2, and 3 together with right sides facing.

To construct bottom of stocking (section 4), hand-appliqué pieces in the following order; G, F, F in reverse, and E (overlapping the other pieces). Appliqué heart and leaves in place and press. As indicated on pattern, attach ribbon to piece E, tacking bow and edges in place. Stitch stocking bottom (section 4) to top (sections 1-2-3), with right sides facing. Pin batting behind stocking piece. Using small outline stitch, hand-stitch around appliquéd pieces through fabric and batting.

From dark red miniprint, cut a 1⅛″ x 6½″ rectangle and sew one long edge (right sides facing) to top edge of section 1. Stitch piping along edge of stocking front, with raw edges aligned. With right sides facing, stitch top of stocking front to top of 1 lining piece and top of stocking back to

top of other lining piece. Press seams open. Lay these pieces with right sides together and stitch, as shown in Diagram 2, leaving opening as indicated. Turn right side out, press, and slipstitch opening closed. Tuck lining into stocking.

From green fabric, cut a 1½″ x 5″ rectangle (for hanger). Fold in half lengthwise, right sides facing, and stitch long edge. Turn right side out and tuck ends in ¼″. Fold in half, forming a loop, and stitch to right-hand corner of stocking.

Diagram 1—Constructing Sections 1, 2, 3, 4, and Appliqué Placement

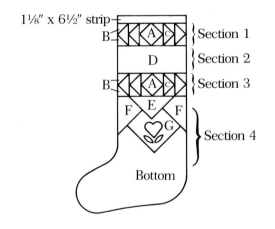

Diagram 2—Stitching Stocking Front and Lining to Stocking Back and Lining

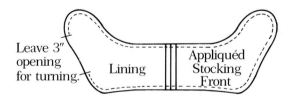

Santa Lives Here

Santa's come to stay. And where Santa hangs this quick-stitch shingle, holiday cheer abounds.

Materials:
patterns begin on page 128
red pindot fabric scrap for hat
white fabric scraps for hatband, hat
  pom-pom, beard, and mustache
water-soluble fabric pen
glue stick
5¼" x 10½" piece of white fabric for
  front
tear-away backing
thread (green, red)
5¼" x 10½" piece of fabric for back
5¼" x 10½" piece of batting
1 yard Christmas print for binding
white quilting thread
brass ring (¾" diameter)
14" (¼"-wide) red pindot ribbon

Transfer hat pattern to red pindot and cut out. Transfer hatband, pom-pom, beard, and mustache patterns to white fabric scraps and cut out. Following photograph, mark mouth on beard with water-soluble fabric pen. Use glue stick to attach pattern pieces to fabric for front. Transfer the words *Santa Lives Here* to front with water-soluble fabric pen.

Cut a piece of tear-away backing same size as front, and pin it to the back of fabric. Machine-embroider words, using satin stitch and green thread. Machine-appliqué hat and beard, using satin stitch and red thread. Machine-stitch mouth, using satin stitch and red thread. Remove tear-away backing.

With fabric right sides out, layer back, batting, and front of hanging and pin together. Machine-stitch around the edges with a ¼" seam.

From Christmas print, cut and stitch together enough 1¼"-wide strips to make 31¾" of bias binding. Fold 1 end under ¼" Beginning with folded end, pin binding to front of hanging, with right sides facing and raw edges aligned. Stitch the binding to the hanging ½" from the edge. Fold the binding to the back, turn the edge under ¼", and blindstitch.

Outline-quilt around hat and beard and inside edge of bias binding. Tack ring to center top of hanging and tie ribbon in a bow at base of the ring.

A Circle of Puppy Love

This wreath is a bounty of bows and doggy bones, and a puppy, fuzzy and festive, peers from the irresistible ring with bright-eyed anticipation.

Materials:
patterns begin on page 128
⅛ yard beige velour fabric (for dog)
scraps of felt (red, white, and black)
  for cap and eyebrows
polyester stuffing
2 (⅓″) black shank-type buttons (for
  eyes)
1 (½″) black shank-type button (for
  nose)
craft glue
½″ red pom-pom (for cap)
6 yards (1¼″-wide) plaid ribbon
1 yard (⅛″-wide) red ribbon
10″ straw wreath
1 yard (2″-wide) red ribbon
small dog treats shaped like bones

Note: Add ¼″ seam allowance to all dog pattern pieces.

Transfer patterns to fabrics indicated and cut out.

For head, body, ears, and paws, with right sides together, stitch around each piece, leaving opening as indicated on patterns. Turn and stuff each piece (except ears); slipstitch openings closed.

Sew ears to head as indicated. For eyes and nose, sew buttons to face as indicated on pattern. Cut tiny strips of black felt (for eyebrows) and glue to face.

Overlap head piece onto body piece, as indicated, and stitch together. Position paws under chin and stitch in place.

For cap: With a ⅛″ seam allowance, stitch around sides leaving bottom edge open. Glue trim to front cap piece. Slipstitch raw edges of cap to head, filling cap with stuffing as you sew. Tack pom-pom to top of cap. Set dog aside.

For bows, fold plaid ribbon to form 2 (2½″) loops, fold again to form 2 more (2½″) loops and pinch together at center. See Diagram. Using short lengths of ⅛″-wide ribbon, tie ribbon tightly around center of bow and knot. Trim ends of bow into V. Make 10 bows. Arrange bows around wreath, leaving a 5″ opening at center bottom; glue bows in place. Glue bones to centers of bows.

Using wide red ribbon and the same steps as above, tie a bow with 3″ loops, and longer ends. Trim ends into a V. Glue bow to center front of wreath at opening. From plaid ribbon, cut 2 (9″) lengths of ribbon, trimming one end of each into a V. Glue straight edges of ribbon behind red bow. Position puppy behind wreath and glue.

Diagram—Making a Bow

A Jolly Reindeer Cookie Carrier

Dressed up in his holiday-best bells and bows, this jovial reindeer is ready to accompany your home-baked goodies to their destination. Once his basket is emptied of its delights, he will happily hold Christmas cards—or some more cookies!

Materials:
patterns begin on page 128
2 squares brown felt
water-soluble fabric marker
1 square white felt
scraps of red felt
thread to match
hot-glue gun and glue sticks
red embroidery floss
stuffing
¼ yard (⅜″-wide) grosgrain ribbon
2 (½″) brass jingle bells
1 (½″) red pom-pom
2 black beads (for eyes)
2 yards (1″-wide) grosgrain ribbon
1 yard (⅛″-wide) satin ribbon
star button
10″ round wicker basket with handle
4 clothespins

Transfer head and arm patterns to brown felt, placing on fold as pattern indicates, and cut out 2 of each piece. Transfer feet pattern to brown felt and cut out 2. Transfer antler pattern to white felt and cut out 4. Transfer inner ear and heart cheeks to red felt and cut out 2 of each.

For each ear, layer and glue 2 small pieces of brown felt and transfer ear pattern to the top piece; do not cut out. Glue inner ear to center of traced ear. Machine-zigzag around inner ear. Cut out ear.

Pin 2 antlers together and, using 2 strands of embroidery floss, handstitch them together, ⅛″ from outside edge, leaving straight edge open for stuffing. Lightly stuff. Repeat procedure for second antler.

Position antlers and ears on back head piece and baste. Pin head pieces together,

with ear/antlers between, and stitch ⅛″ from outside edge, leaving an opening at bottom. Stuff head and stitch closed. Referring to photograph for placement, handstitch a 2½″ length of ⅜″ ribbon across face. Turn ribbon ends under at sides of face and tack in place. Sew jingle bells to ribbon ends.

For eyes and nose, stitch beads and glue pom-pom to face. Using 2 strands of floss, backstitch a smile. Glue red hearts at ends of smile. Make bow with remaining ⅜″ ribbon and glue at base of ear. Cut a 12″ piece of 1″-wide ribbon and loop twice to form a bow. Stitch to reindeer's chin area and sew button at center.

Pin 2 arm pieces together and stitch ⅛″ from outside edge, leaving an opening. Lightly stuff arms and stitch closed. Repeat procedure with feet.

Glue arms and feet, opposite each other, to outside of basket. Use clothespins to secure until glue dries. Place head inside basket edge, at center of arms, and glue.

Cut satin ribbon and remaining grosgrain ribbon in half. For each bow, make 2 loops with a length of grosgrain ribbon and, using satin ribbon, tie to basket handle where it meets the basket. Make bow with ends of satin ribbon. Cut V in ribbon ends.

Merry Mouse Card Holder

A gift-toting mouse masquerading as Santa stands guard over Christmas greetings from neighbors and friends. Cross-stitched on a large mesh cloth, this design works up quickly. Below the mouse is a spacious striped pocket to hold the salutations of the season.

Materials:
charts begin on page 128
10″ x 18″ piece 6-count ecru Herta cloth
embroidery floss (see color key)
#20 tapestry needle
18″ (¼″-wide) Christmas print ribbon
craft glue
10″ x 6″ piece Christmas print fabric
2 (3″ x 8″) strips matching Christmas print fabric
10″ x 18″ piece unbleached muslin
small jingle bell

Center design on width of Herta cloth, beginning 1¼″ down from the top edge, and work according to chart. Use 6 strands of floss to cross-stitch. Use 4 strands for backstitch that outlines mouse and for long-stitch to make whiskers and fringe.

Thread ribbon through tapestry needle and weave through cloth over package as indicated on chart. Trim excess ribbon and tack ends to fabric back to secure. Tie remaining ribbon in a bow and set aside.

To hem top edge of pocket, fold one long edge of 10″ x 6″ print fabric ¼″ to wrong side, fold under again, and press. Stitch close to folded edge. With right sides together and raw edges aligned, lay Christmas fabric on top of Herta cloth. Baste together along side and bottom edges.

For hanger loops, fold one 3″ x 8″ strip in half lengthwise with right sides facing and raw edges aligned. Stitch together along long edge with a ¼″ seam. Turn. Press, centering seam. Repeat with remaining fabric strip.

Fold one strip in half with raw edges aligned and seam inside. Pin raw edges to top edge of right side of Herta cloth, ¼″ from side edge. Baste in place. Repeat with remaining strip.

With right sides together and raw edges aligned, pin muslin to Herta cloth. Using a ¼″ seam and leaving an opening for turning, stitch pieces together. Remove pins and turn. Press. Blindstitch opening closed.

Tack jingle bell to mouse's cap. Glue ribbon bow under mouse's chin.

Snowdrift Tree Skirt

Make a pretty snowdrift under your tree with this white polished-cotton skirt. The color scheme, a white field accented with fat little red and green hearts, hints of nature's vivid scenery: A snow-covered pine bough visited by a crimson cardinal, feathers puffed against the cold.

Materials:
patterns begin on page 128
6¾ yards (45″-wide) white polished cotton fabric
3½ yards polyester batting
⅜ yard (45″-wide) red miniprint fabric (for hearts)
¼ yard (45″-wide) white print fabric (for hearts)
3½ yards (45″-wide) dark green fabric
3″ (½″-wide) black Velcro
3″ (½″-wide) white Velcro
1 yard (⅛″-wide) elastic
7½ yards (½″-wide) white satin ribbon
14 yards (⅛″-wide) dark green satin ribbon
3½ yards (⅛″-wide) red satin ribbon
10½ yards (⅜″-wide) dark green satin ribbon
dressmakers' pen
polyester stuffing

For tree skirt, from white fabric cut 4 (45″ x 60″) rectangles. Using ½″ seam allowance, stitch 2 rectangles together, (right sides facing) along 60″ selvage edges. (Do not open piece up.) Fold seamed unit in half to form quarters (45″ x 30″); pin together. Working from corner with folded and seamed sides, draw arcs with 3″ and 30″ radiuses. (See Diagram.) Mark with dressmakers' pen. Cut through all layers to make skirt top. To make center back opening of tree skirt, remove stitching from seam in one half of unit.

To make lining, repeat above steps for remaining rectangle pieces.

Cut batting into 2 (45″ x 60″) rectangles. Whipstitch the 2 rectangles together along one half of 60″ edge. Using skirt top as a pattern, cut batting.

Transfer heart pattern to fabrics and, from red miniprint, cut 28 hearts. From white print, cut 14 hearts. Set aside.

To make underskirt, from green fabric, cut two rectangles (45″x 60″) and repeat top skirt instructions. Machine-stitch a narrow hem around all edges. From black Velcro, cut 3 (1″) strips. At three equal intervals, sew loop side of strips to one edge of center back opening (right side) and hook side of strips to opposite edge (wrong side). Set underskirt aside.

Layer pieces in the following order; batting piece, lining piece (right side up), and skirt top (right side down). Pin layers together securely. Using ¼″ seam allowance, stitch down one edge of back opening, around entire outside edge, and up opposite edge of opening, leaving inside circle open. Trim batting from seam allowance; clip corners and turn through inside circle opening. Fold seam allowance under around inside circle opening and slipstitch closed. From white Velcro, cut 3 (1″) strips. To close center back opening, attach Velcro

Diagram—Cutting Layout

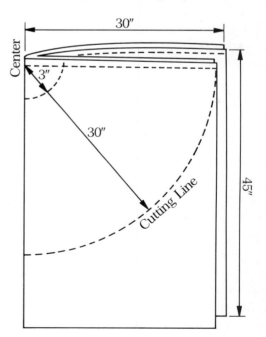

strips as for underskirt.

To divide tree skirt into 8 equal portions: Use dressmakers' pen to make marks 2⅓" apart around edge of inside circle and 23½" apart around outside edge. Draw straight lines between marks. Machine-stitch down each line to quilt skirt and secure layers.

From elastic, cut 9 (4") strips. On the wrong side of tree skirt, measure up 8½" from outside edge at every quilting line and both opening edges and make a mark. Secure elastic strips to quilting lines at outside edge, securing the other ends to 8½" marks. Zigzag over each piece of elastic without catching it in stitching.

From white ribbon, cut 9 (30") lengths. Fold ½" of 1 ribbon under and, on wrong side of skirt, stitch ½" below inner circle edge. Bring ribbon over edge to skirt front and topstitch down both sides of ribbon to beginning of elastic. Wrap remaining ribbon loosely over gathered area to point at which elastic begins on wrong side. Fold under ribbon end and stitch. Repeat for remaining ribbons.

With right sides facing, stitch matching hearts together to make 14 red miniprint and 7 white print hearts. Clip inside corners and curved seam allowances. Turn

and stuff lightly. Slipstitch openings closed.

From ⅛"-wide green ribbon, cut 14 (5") lengths and 42 (10") lengths. Set 14 (10") lengths aside for white hearts. For each red heart, tack one end of a 5" length to the center top. Handling 2 (10") lengths as one, tie into 2½"-wide bow. Tack bow to center top of heart. Repeat for remaining red hearts.

From red ribbon, cut 7 (7") lengths and 7 (10") lengths. Tack one end of a 7" length ribbon to center top of each white heart. Place 2 green and 1 red 10" length together. Handling as one, tie into 2½"-wide bow. Tack to center top of heart. Repeat for remaining white hearts.

Make 7 units of 2 red hearts and 1 white heart, suspended at slightly different lengths. Knot ribbons together 5" from white heart in each group. Tack knot 16½" from edge of inside circle, centered over white ribbon.

From ⅜" green ribbon, cut 14 (18") lengths and 14 (9") lengths. Handling 2 (18") lengths as one, fold into 5"-wide loops. Handling 2 (9") lengths as one, tie around center of loops. Repeat for remaining ribbon lengths. Tack bows over knots of hanging hearts.

54

A Cozy Cottage Says Welcome

Delve into your scrap bag for the raw materials to build this house. Mix and match fabrics for a striped roof, a polka-dot tree, or a calico chimney. Then machine-appliqué this picturesque wall hanging to give a warm greeting.

Materials:
patterns begin on page 128
1 yard unbleached muslin
½ yard lightweight iron-on interfacing
Christmas print fabric scraps
matching thread
fusible web
7″ (⅜″-wide) flat lace
craft glue
½ yard polyester batting
tissue paper
water-soluble marking pen
green paint pen
12″ length of (¼″) wooden dowel
2 (¼″-hole) red wooden beads
½ yard (1″-wide) striped grosgrain
ribbon

Note: A ministripe print for the roof will make channel quilting easier.

From muslin, cut out sign pattern 2 times. Back 1 sign piece and all appliqué fabrics with iron-on interfacing. Transfer patterns to fabrics and cut one of each appliqué piece from colors shown in the photograph.

Position house, roof, and tree on muslin background. Place pieces of web (smaller than patterns) in between. Fuse in place. Appliqué with wide satin stitch.

Position shrub, door, chimney, window, and shutters, and fuse in place with small pieces of web as above. Appliqué with medium satin stitch. Continue fusing remaining pieces in the following order; door window, tulips, cobblestone steps, and heart window. Appliqué with narrow satin stitch. As indicated on pattern, topstitch

window panes and door window with contrasting thread and stitch lace trim to roof. For a doorknob, cut a medallion from the lace trim and glue in place. Or substitute a button and stitch it to the door.

Hand-baste batting to appliquéd muslin piece. Place tissue paper beneath batting. Machine-stitch an outline around appliquéd pieces and channel-quilt roof.

Using water-soluble marking pen, print "WELCOME TO THE ......" (inserting your last name). (To erase imperfect printing, wet fabric and rinse ink out thoroughly, let dry completely, and print again.) Write over printing with paint pen. Allow to dry and machine-quilt over printing.

Using a wide satin stitch, stitch in red around the bottom edge of the sign. Clip threads; tear off tissue paper from back of piece and discard. Remove basting stitches.

Pin plain muslin piece to appliquéd muslin piece with right sides facing. Stitch around perimeter with ¼″ seam allowance, leaving a 2 ½″ opening at bottom (for turning) and a 1″ opening at top corner of each side (for dowel). Trim seam, clip curves, and turn right side out. Slipstitch bottom opening closed and lightly press.

Insert dowel between backing and batting and glue red wooden beads to ends. Tie ribbon to ends for hanging.

A Cowboy Christmas

The Christmas Cowboy and his trusty steed, Ribbons, will lasso your heart. With a broad smile and a dashing bandanna, this cowboy is certainly one of the good guys. His ten-gallon hat is shaped from felt. The beribboned rocking horse gallops atop a small embroidery hoop. Snippets of scrap-bag materials shape these ornaments.

ROCKING HORSE
Materials:
patterns begin on page 128
4″ wooden embroidery hoop
6″ circle of white and green pindot
6″ square of red Christmas fabric
4½″ x 2″ length of green felt
4″ square of heavy poster board
3″ square batting
craft glue
2 (¼″) gold buttons
1″ square of red felt
2″ (⅛″-wide) green satin ribbon
fabric stiffener
1½ yards (⅛″-wide) red satin ribbon
⅛″ wooden dowel
½ yard (¾″-wide) red flat trim

Cut out patterns as indicated.

Open hoop and place circle of fabric right side up on top of smaller hoop. Replace top hoop and close fastener, adjusting fabric to fit smoothly. Glue fabric to the bottom of the hoop to secure. Glue rocker in place along the bottom inside edge of the hoop (see photograph).

To make the horse: Glue the poster board body to batting body. Place fabric body right side down and center board body on top with batting side down. Apply glue to edge of plain side of board, and, clipping curves, wrap fabric around edge, and glue to secure. Prepare legs the same way, excluding batting. Glue the top of each leg to body and glue a button at top of each leg. Cut a small heart from red felt and glue near the curved bottom of the saddle. For stirrup, make a loop with green

ribbon and glue to wrong side of saddle, with loop extending ½″ below bottom. Glue the saddle to the horse, wrapping the straight end over the back of the horse. Glue the horse to the embroidery hoop, leaving an opening for the ribbon tail.

To make mane and tail: Pour equal amounts of water and stiffener into a cup. Cut a 9″ length from the red ribbon. Submerge remainder of ribbon in the stiffener solution. Run ribbon between fingers to squeeze out excess stiffener. Tape one end of ribbon to wooden dowel and wind ribbon around dowel, making a tight coil. Tape other end of ribbon to dowel when finished. Let ribbon dry overnight; remove tape and unwind from dowel. Cut 3 (1¼″) lengths of curled ribbon, bunch them closely together, and glue under open tail area. Glue the remainder of the ribbon on the head for the mane.

Beginning at hoop closure, turn end of flat trim under and glue trim along the outside edge of the hoop. Thread the 9″ length of red ribbon through hoop closure and tie in a knot.

CHRISTMAS COWBOY
Materials:
patterns begin on page 128
2 (6″ square) pieces heavy cardboard
2 (6″ square) pieces batting
2 (6″ square) pieces pink cotton fabric
9″ x 11″ piece medium brown felt
craft glue
¼ yard (½″-wide) white flat trim with red hearts
8″ length gold thread
dark brown yarn
1 (6″-square) piece green check fabric
green thread
4″ square red felt
6″ of red yarn
4 black (8-mm) beads
2 (¼″) pink pom-poms

Note: Ornament is reversible; seam allowances are ¼″ unless indicated.

To make face: Trace and cut out 2 ovals

56

each from cardboard and batting. Glue a batting oval to each board oval. Add ½" all around pattern and cut out 2 pink fabric ovals. Place fabric ovals right side down with board ovals, batting side down, on top. Make ½" slashes around the pink fabric ovals and glue to the plain side of cardboard. Glue the board ovals together with the fabric sides out.

To make hat: Stitch darts in crowns with a ⅛" seam. With right sides together, sew the crown pieces together along the sides and top. Turn right side out. Stitch brim circles together around edges. Fold in half and slash along fold, beginning and ending slash ¾" from edge. Turn brim right side out and press. Fit hat crown over "top" of face oval, and glue to hold. Slide the brim over the crown, aligning the bottom edge of the crown and the center cut of the brim. Glue in place. Glue trim around hat to cover edges where crown and brim join. Turn up sides of brim and glue to hold. Sew a loop of gold thread to the top of the hat for a hanger.

To make hair: Wind the brown yarn around 3 fingers, 20 times. Gently slide loops off fingers, and tie in center. Repeat for second hair bundle. Glue one bundle to each side of the face, tucking the hair under the hat brim.

To make scarf: Fold green fabric square in half on the diagonal. With right sides together, sew ¼" seam, leaving opening for turning; turn right side out. Press under a ¼" hem on raw edge, but do not stitch together. Wind matching thread 1½" from corners at ends of raw edge, to give the appearance that scarf has been tied. Slide the open edge of the scarf up over the bottom of the chin about ½" and glue in place.

To make facial features: Cut 4 small hearts from red felt. Cut 2 (2") lengths from red yarn. On each face, glue the red yarn in place for the smile and glue the hearts in place for the cheeks. Glue pompom noses and bead eyes in place on each face (see photograph).

57

A Ruffled Wreath Made to Last

Frilly ruffles ring this wreath. But look again. Although it appears fluffy, this wreath is hard and durable, thanks to the amazing material that shapes it. So don't worry when you store your wreath at season's end. Its ruffles will stay fresh for years to come.

Materials:
patterns begin on page 128
6 yards (40″-wide) Dip 'N Drape fabric
scissors
14″ straw wreath
1 (13″) piece of wire
5″ x 10″ piece of thin corrugated cardboard
craft knife
craft glue (optional)
drill with small bit
gesso
paintbrush
white gloss spray paint
acrylic paint (red, green)
small (no. 00) artists' brush
clear gloss spray
14″ (¼″-wide) green ribbon

Note: Dip 'N Drape fabric is coated with a substance that, when wet, can be shaped with your fingers. It dries very hard and, after an application of gesso, can be decoratively painted. Dip 'N Drape is available in many craft shops or can be ordered through Zim's. For information write:

Zim's, 4370 South 300 West, P.O. Box 7620, Salt Lake City, UT 84107.

Cut 7 (2″ x 20″) strips from fabric. Run strips quickly through water one at a time. Pull strips between fingers to squeeze out excess water; wrap through center opening and around wreath to cover it.

To make hanger, run wire through center opening and around wreath, twisting ends together. Twist wire ends into a loop at back of wreath.

Cut 37 (5″ x 20″) strips to make ruffles. Fold strips in half lengthwise. To make a ruffle, dip and prepare fabric as above. Press one end of strip to back of wreath, gathering the fabric as you apply it, and press raw edge to wreath as you move around it. Overlap ends and press flat at back of wreath.

Be sure to keep first ruffle raised so that last ruffle applied can be tucked under it. Each new row should overlap previous row enough to hide raw edges. Apply no more than 5 or 6 ruffles at a time, allowing each section to dry and harden before adding the next section.

Using pattern and craft knife, cut two hearts from cardboard; then cut two from fabric, adding ⅜″ all around. Prepare fabric hearts as above. Clip curves and cover one side of each cardboard heart with a fabric heart, wrapping raw edges smoothly to back. Set aside and let dry. For ruffle, cut one (2″ x 20″) strip of fabric and fold in half lengthwise. Wet and prepare fabric strip as above. Beginning at top, apply raw edges of strip to back of one heart, gathering all around to make a ruffle. (Ruffle should extend ¾″ out from heart.) Press hearts together, back to back. The damp fabric should stick the two hearts together. (If necessary, add a little glue to center back of heart.) Let dry.

Drill a small hole through ruffle at center top of heart. With paintbrush, paint gesso on top sides of ruffles on wreath and on both sides of heart, including ruffle. Let dry. Apply two coats white spray paint to wreath and to both sides of heart. Let dry. Using artists' brush, paint crossed lines and dot designs on ruffles, reversing use of red and green on each successive ruffle. (See photograph.) Paint heart as shown on pattern. Let dry.

Spray wreath and heart with clear gloss spray. Let dry. Run ribbon through hole in heart and hang from wire hanger on wreath so that heart is suspended in center of wreath.

Ski Bunny
Takes to the Slopes

This spunky ski bunny, shown as a tree ornament, is also our cover model. A white sock, stitched and stuffed in strategic places, is transformed into a respectable rabbit. Colorful knee socks make ski togs, and skis and poles are crafted from popsicle sticks and picks.

Materials:
patterns begin on page 128
1 women's (size 9-11) white brushed-nylon lounge sock
water-soluble marker
matching thread
2 pipe cleaners
white carpet or button thread
polyester stuffing
long embroidery needle
embroidery floss (light blue, medium pink)
1 women's (size 9-11) striped knee sock (for pants and hat)
½ yard (⅜"-wide) grosgrain ribbon (for suspenders)
2 (½") white pom-poms
hot-glue gun and glue sticks
9" x ⅝" scrap of wool fabric (for scarf)
2 popsicle sticks (for skis)
2 (3½") round wooden picks (for ski poles)
acrylic paint (red, white)
small craft paintbrush
needlenose pliers with cutting edge
¼ yard thin gold elastic cord

Note: Backstitch at beginning and end of every seam. Pants and hat may need to be adjusted to fit the bunny.

Turn sock inside out and flatten, with heel seams matching. Cut away any elastic cuff. Referring to Diagram 1, transfer body pattern to sock and machine-stitch along marked line. Cut ⅛" outside of seam line and save remainder of sock for arm and leg pieces.

For ears, turn body piece wrong side out. Flatten body piece with seam centered and facing up. (Refer to Diagram 2.) Make a ½" mark on the center seam, 4" up from open end. Stitch down one side of center seam from toe to mark; then stitch along mark and back up other side of center seam to toe. Clip between ear seams from toe to just above cross seam. Trim tips of ears and turn entire piece right side out.

Cut pipe cleaners 1" longer than ear length. Insert a pipe cleaner from bottom of body until tip reaches the end of one ear. Wrap carpet thread around base of ear (securing pipe cleaner inside), pull tightly, knot thread, and clip. Repeat for other ear.

Stuff evenly until body piece is about 3½" long and 5½" in circumference. Tuck raw edges inside and whipstitch opening closed.

To form head, wrap thread several times around stuffed body (about 1½" from ear base). Pull thread tightly to make neck indention; knot thread twice and clip. (Head should be the size of a golf ball.) To form legs and arms, trim remaining sock piece into a 3″ x 7½″ rectangle. With right side facing up, fold short ends to meet at center and pin. Machine-stitch 4 seams down the length of folded piece, as shown in Diagram 3. Stitch first seam ¼″ in from one long raw edge, second seam ⅝″ away from the first, third seam ½″ from the second seam, and fourth seam ⅝″ from the third seam. Cut between second and third seams to form two pieces. Cut each piece across at point where short ends meet in the center. (Refer to Diagram 3.) Trim seam allowances. These four pieces are the arms and legs. Turn right side out and stuff.

For legs, turn raw edges in and slipstitch to body base. For arms, turn raw edges in and slipstitch closed. Thread needle with approximately 2 feet of thread and knot end. Hold arms in position on body sides at shoulders, insert needle in center of one arm piece at shoulder area and push through body, exiting through arm piece and shoulder area on other side. Repeat pass-through step several times, pulling thread firmly to secure arms. Exit needle between arm and body at shoulder. Knot securely and clip.

To form face, thread needle with approximately 2 feet of thread and knot end. (See Diagram 4.) Insert needle at neck in back of head and exit at point 1. Take a small stitch and re-enter at point 1, exiting through point 2. Take a small stitch and re-enter at point 2, exiting through point 1. Pull thread gently to form eye sockets and nose ridge. (Do not indent too deeply.) For chin dimple re-enter at point 1 and exit at point 3. Take a ¼″ stitch over fabric and enter at point 4. Exit at point 2; taking a small stitch, re-enter at point 2 and exit at point 4. Take a stitch over fabric, entering at point 3 and exiting at point 1. Pull thread firmly to form chin dimple. Secure thread at point 1 and re-enter at point 1 exiting at top of head. Clip thread.

For eyes, using 3 strands of blue floss, insert needle in neck indention at back of head and exit at one eye socket. Using

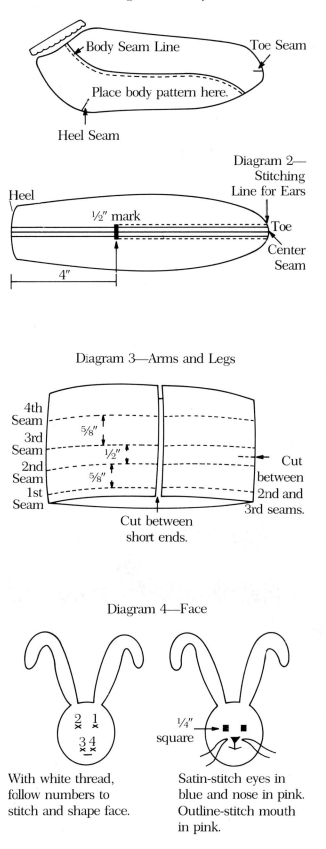

Diagram 1—Body

Body Seam Line

Toe Seam

Place body pattern here.

Heel Seam

Diagram 2—
Stitching
Line for Ears

Heel

½″ mark

Toe

Center Seam

4″

Diagram 3—Arms and Legs

4th Seam

3rd Seam

2nd Seam

1st Seam

⅝″

½″

⅝″

Cut between 2nd and 3rd seams.

Cut between short ends.

Diagram 4—Face

2 1
x x

3 4
x x

With white thread, follow numbers to stitch and shape face.

¼″ square

Satin-stitch eyes in blue and nose in pink. Outline-stitch mouth in pink.

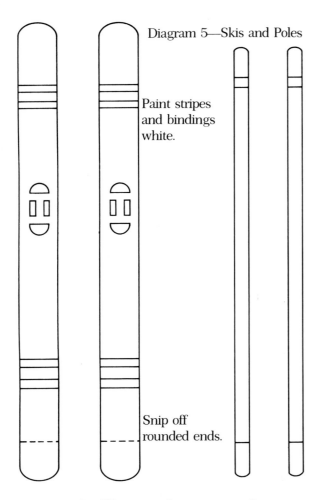

Diagram 5—Skis and Poles

Paint stripes and bindings white.

Snip off rounded ends.

satin stitch, fill in a ¼″ square in the eye socket area. When completed, insert needle into eye corner, exit through top of head, and clip the thread without knotting. Repeat for second eye.

For nose, using 3 strands of pink floss and satin stitch, insert needle in back neck indention, exiting at nose ridge. Embroider a triangular shape for nose. Form the mouth using outline stitch. (See Diagram 4.) Secure thread at base of nose and exit needle through top of head. Clip thread.

For whiskers, double-thread a needle with white thread and knot together, approximately 2″ from ends. Insert needle on one side of nose and exit on opposite side, pulling thread until knot rests snugly against nose. Knot thread, making sure second knot rests against other side of nose. Clip thread, leaving a 2″ tail. Trim whiskers to equal length.

For pants and hat, cut ribbing off knee sock and turn inside out. Flatten sock, matching heel seams, and transfer patterns to calf part of sock, placing pattern sides on folds as indicated. (Width of sock will affect pattern placement.) Before cutting out pieces, stitch seams as marked. Cut out pieces, leaving ¼″ seam allowances at pants waist and legs, and ⅛″ on all other edges. Turn right side out. (Be careful not to unravel raw edges.) Pull pants on bunny. Turn pants leg edges and waist under ¼″ and hem. Hand-stitch pants legs to bunny legs.

For suspenders, cut ribbon into two equal lengths. Using photograph as guide for placement, tuck ends of ribbon under pants waist, crossing in back. Hand-stitch pants to bunny body at waist, securing the suspenders.

For the hat, fold hat flat with seam centered on bottom. On one side, measure up 1″ and clip a ¼″ slit for ear. Repeat on other side. Carefully pull ears through slits and adjust hat to fit bunny head. Tuck raw edges of hat under and slipstitch in place. Hot-glue the pom-poms, one to top of hat and one to back of bunny's pants.

For the scarf, at each short end of the wool scrap, pull out the cross threads until fringe is about ¼″ long. Tie scarf around the neck.

For skis and poles, paint all sides of popsicle sticks and picks red. Let paint dry. Using Diagram 5 as a guide, paint white stripes and bindings on skis and poles. When dry, use pliers to snip off one rounded end from each ski. Glue skis and poles together in X position. (Refer to photograph.) Position skis on arm so that hand folds over skis slightly. To hot-glue in place, fold bunny's hand over ski when gluing and hold in place for a few seconds. Repeat steps for poles in other hand. A variation for an action bunny; glue skis onto feet and secure one pole in each hand.

For hanger, thread needle with gold cord and attach at back of hat.

62

A Winter Wonderland Under Your Tree

For a winter wonderland under your tree, appliqué lace snowflakes onto soft blue fabric triangles. Then join the geometric shapes to form this winter-sky tree skirt.

Materials:
patterns, diagrams begin on page 128
1 square yard paper for patterns
4 yards (45″-wide) 100% cotton blue-and-white print fabric
4 yards (45″-wide) muslin
1 full-size (81″ x 96″) polyester quilt batt
1½ yards (60″-wide) polyester blend tablecloth lace
thread to match fabrics
190″ cording (optional)

Note: All seam allowances are ½″ unless otherwise indicated.

To make a triangle pattern, construct an equilateral triangle with 33″ sides. Draw a line across the triangle 2½″ down from 1 top corner (see Diagram).

Preshrink fabrics, remove selvages, and iron. Cut 6 triangles from blue fabric, 6 from muslin, and 6 from batting.

Transfer ½ of the snowflake pattern to paper. Cut six snowflakes from folded lace.

Mark the center line of each blue triangle by folding lengthwise in half and finger creasing. Center 1 folded snowflake along this line so that its points are 1″ from the triangle's base and side edges. Open snowflake and pin in place. Lay the blue triangle on a batting triangle and pin edges. Using white thread, machine-baste the snowflake to blue fabric and batting along all edges. Repeat for all 6 triangles.

Set machine for a medium-wide zigzag and stitch all edges of the 6 snowflakes.

To form the large hexagon, pin 2 blue triangles, right sides together, pushing the batting out of the way as you pin. Stitch along 1 edge and press seam open. Smooth batting edges over the seam and trim them

to lie flat. Use large stitches to baste batting edges together by hand. Sew remaining triangles together in the same way, leaving one edge unsewn for closure.

If a corded edge is desired, cut and sew together enough 1¾″ bias strips from blue fabric to make a 190″ strip. With cording in fold of bias strip, use zipper foot to stitch close to cording. Pin piping to right side of the tree skirt's outer edge, matching raw edges. Stitch through all layers, clipping curves where needed.

To make ties for closure, cut 4 strips of blue fabric, 14″ x 1½″. Fold long raw edges to meet in center; then fold lengthwise again. Sew down center of tie with a zigzag stitch. Knot one end of each tie. Pin other ends to the back openings of tree skirt near top and bottom, matching raw edges. Sew over the ties several times, ¼″ from raw edges.

Make the skirt lining by sewing the six muslin triangles together, leaving one edge unsewn. With right sides together, pin the lining to the tree skirt and sew around all edges of the skirt, leaving an 8″ opening at one back edge to turn. Turn right side out and press. Sew opening closed by hand.

Using blue thread, topstitch (machine-quilt) all edges of the tree skirt; then stitch ¼″ away from all edges of snowflakes.

Jolly Little Christmas Elf

Mischievous Mick brings the luck of the Irish to your festivities. His penchant for green shows in a felt vest (over Christmas stripes) and matching elfin shoes and hat, a-jingle with bells. Button eyes twinkle in a soft velour face framed by a wild red-yarn beard. With the help of a little bird, Mick strings popcorn.

Materials:
patterns begin on page 128
6″ x 20″ piece of flesh-colored velour fabric
polyester stuffing
2 (³⁄₈″) black, half-round, shank-type buttons
red yarn
4 jingle bells
¼ yard red-striped stretch fabric
4 (9″ x 12″) pieces of green felt
4 (¼″) white, half round, shank-type buttons
metallic gold rickrack
1 yard metallic gold cording
1″ holly trim
small white feather
popcorn
1½″ craft bird

Note: Use ¼″ seam allowance unless otherwise indicated.

Fold flesh fabric piece in half, with 6″ edges aligned and right sides together. Transfer head and ear patterns to fabric, as marked, but do not cut out. Leaving open where indicated, stitch around each piece, through both layers of fabric. Cut out pieces, leaving ¼″ seam allowance. Turn. Stuff head firmly and slipstitch openings closed.

Fold lobe of ear pieces up ½″. Position tucked ears with lobes toward the face and tip of ears pointing up; pin to back head piece, ¼″ from side seam, as indicated, and slipstitch in place.

Transfer nose pattern to flesh fabric and cut 1. Hand-sew small running stitches around nose piece ¼″ from outer edges. Pull thread slightly to gather. Stuff nose, pull thread tightly to close opening, and knot. Stitch nose to face. For eyes, sew two black buttons where indicated.

To make beard, wrap yarn around 2 fingers 10 times, slip off and tie a piece of yarn around center of bundle. Make enough bundles to cover the face from beard line down to chin as indicated on pattern. For eyebrows, tack ¼″ scraps of red yarn above eyes, as indicated on pattern. Sew a bell on each ear lobe.

For the body and legs, fold red-striped fabric in half, 9″ edges aligned and right sides together. Transfer patterns to fabric. Leaving openings where indicated, stitch around pieces. Cut out, leaving ¼″ seam allowance. Turn pieces right side out and stuff firmly. Fold raw edges of legs under ¼″ and slipstitch to body as indicated on pattern.

Transfer hand pattern to flesh fabric and arm pattern to striped fabric. Cut 2 of each, on the fold. Sew 1 hand piece to 1 arm piece, right sides together, with raw edge of wrist and end of arm piece aligned. Fold lengthwise, right sides facing, and stitch, leaving arm end open. Repeat for remaining arm/hand pieces. Turn right side out and stuff firmly. Fold raw edges of arms under ¼″ and slipstitch to body. Slipstitch head to body.

For clothing, transfer hat, vest front and back, and shoe patterns to green felt, as marked, and cut out. For hat, with right sides facing, machine-stitch pieces together, leaving bottom edge open. Trim seams. Stitch rickrack to wrong side of hat along trim line. Turn hat right side out and turn edge up to fold line. Pin hat to head, with seams at sides, and slipstitch to head. Fold point of hat to one side of head and tack behind ear.

Hold vest front and back pieces up to body and check fit, adjusting if necessary. Tack vest front and back pieces to body at

shoulders. Overlap vest front tabs on vest back at sides and sew a white button on each tab. Sew 2 buttons on vest front.

For shoes, machine-stitch two pieces together along heel. Trim seam, open piece, and stitch rickrack to wrong side of shoe, ¼″ from top edge. Fold shoe in half at heel seam, right sides together and edges aligned, and stitch around shoe, leaving top open. Turn to right side and hand-sew a running stitch ¼″ down from rickrack. Do

not cut thread. Place shoe on foot, pull thread to gather snugly around ankle, and knot. Repeat for other shoe. Stitch a bell to each shoe toe. Cut gold cord in half, tie into 2 bows, and tack one to top of each shoe. Turn down cuffs.

Tack holly trim and feather behind one ear. String popcorn on red thread; tack one end to a hand and the other to bird beak. Tack bird to other hand. Cross one leg over the other and tack to hold.

Gild Your Tree with Golden Sleds

Stitch festive sayings on sled ornaments for zippy symbols of winter fun.

Materials:
patterns begin on page 128
2 golden sled ornaments from
Needleforms
#24 tapestry needle
embroidery floss (see color key)
14″ (⅛″-wide) red satin ribbon

Work one design on each sled according to charts. Use 3 strands of floss for cross-stitch and 3 strands of black for letters on Santa design. Use 1 strand of black to backstitch the outline of Santa. Use 3 strands of floss for all cross-stitch of the Noel design.

Use 7″ of red ribbon for each hanger. Thread ribbon ends through holes at top of sled and knot them to secure.

Ornamental Hexagons Banded with Color

Striking in their simple, clean geometry, these gleaming hexagonal ornaments are both sophisticated and festive. Banded in bright, bold colors with glints of gold and silver, they are stunning whether presented alone, as a set, or suspended from a mobile. And they are a snap to make.

You will need a 3″ x 7″ piece of lightweight cardboard, straight pins with plastic heads, and a total of 24 yards of thread for each ornament (#5 pearl cotton and metallic thread of a similar weight were used here).

Transfer the pattern (see page 128) to the cardboard and cut out. Mark triangles with letters, arrows, and numbers as indicated. Using a craft knife, lightly score fold lines. Fold the pattern, folding top points of Triangles A, B, and C toward each other, forming a pyramid. Tape edges with transparent tape. Repeat procedure with Triangles D, E, and F.

Insert a pin in each of the 5 corners, applying a bead of glue under pin head to secure. Let dry.

Make a slipknot at end of thread and place around the pin at the top of Triangle A. Referring to Diagram and following

numbers and arrows, wind thread around pins. Turn the ornament as you wind, holding the thread firmly and keeping tension even. Continue winding thread, laying strands next to each other, covering cardboard.

To make a stripe, cut end of wrapped thread and glue to cardboard where there is a single layer of thread. Glue new thread to end of old and continue wrapping.

For hanger, tie a length of yarn to the pin at the top of Triangle A.

Diagram—Wrapping Thread

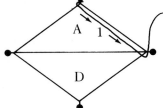 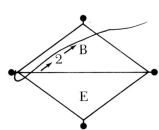 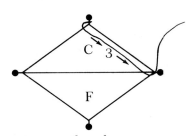

Knot thread around pin at top of triangle A. Follow numbers and arrows to wrap thread, turning the ornament as thread is wound around ornament.

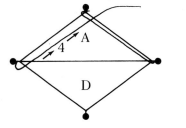 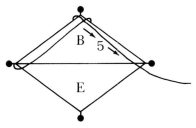

Place Mats That Mirror the Excitement Of the Season

Razzle dazzle. It's part of the excitement of the season, and it can be yours surprisingly simply. Purchased place mats become the canvas, and fabric cutouts and metallic fabric paint form the palette.

The look here is stylishly contemporary, ready for an elegant New Year's Eve supper, but the technique can yield as many types of mats as there are settings for them. You might want to use scraps left over from decorating your dining room, fabric emblazoned with the colors of the season, or even bits of a worn-out evening dress! The key is imagination.

When choosing fabrics and fabric glue, check cleaning directions. All should require compatible treatment. Some glues can take several dry cleanings, but can't take washing.

To prolong the number of uses between cleanings, you might want to treat the mats with spray fabric protector. Just be sure to test scraps of all fabrics first, and follow manufacturer's directions.

Once fabrics and glue have been selected, it's time to set about creatively combining the materials. With this mat, an abstract black shape was glued in place first. The next step was to cut a printed flower and a whimsical leaf from coordinating fabrics. Leaf, then flower, were glued into place and allowed to dry.

Next, all shapes were outlined using a small brush and silver metallic fabric paint. When you outline, don't worry if your lines vary in thickness. As you can see here, that's part of the charm.

These mats are naturals for gifts, bazaars, and your own home. Take the technique another step, and use a strip of the appliqué fabric to tie around napkins. You might also appliqué a frame for a centerpiece on a matching tablecloth. A vase of flowers placed on a glittering base of fabrics is sure to draw a round of admiration.

A Wreath for All Seasons

This unusually handsome wreath, an accessory for any season, is made of clustered strips of fiber rush. The material is a warm brown color, but here it is tipped in deep red, an accent obtained by dipping the twisted rush strips in dye.

Materials:
12″ or 14″ Styrofoam or straw wreath
  form
1 package fabric dye in color desired
10 yards (³⁄₁₆″) fiber rush
10 yards (⁵⁄₃₂″) fiber rush
rubber gloves
hot-glue gun and glue sticks
scrap of twine

Mix dye with hot water in a large container. Allow to cool. Cut ³⁄₁₆″ (10 yards) rush into 5-yard lengths. Gently untwist and smooth one length and, wearing rubber gloves, dye this length, soaking for 1 to 2 minutes. Hang outside and allow to dry.

Dye the remaining lengths (5 yards of ³⁄₁₆″ and 10 yards of ⁵⁄₃₂″) without untwisting. Hang outside to dry.

Firmly wrap wreath form with the untwisted rush, completely covering it. Secure ends of rush with hot glue.

Untwist the remaining ³⁄₁₆″ (5 yards) rush and form a large bow (see Diagram), tying twine through the bow loops to secure them. Glue the bow to the wreath at the six o'clock position.

For rush "leaves," cut the ⁵⁄₃₂″ (10 yards) twisted rush into 6″- to 7″-long strips. Carefully untwist each strip, beginning in the center and leaving about ½″ of each end twisted. For each leaf cluster, glue 2 strips together at their centers, forming a cross. While glue is still damp, pinch intersection of leaves to form 4 leaf-shaped petals and bend petals up to form cluster. Glue the cluster to the wreath. Repeat procedure until the front of the wreath is covered.

Diagram—Making a Bow

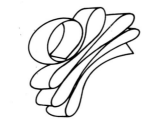 

Separate loops for a fluffy bow.

A Jolly Pair

Kris and Mrs. Kringle exude good cheer with their Christmassy apparel and sweet faces haloed by frosty white hair. The dolls are basic shapes, but the ingenious trims—such as Mrs. Kringle's tin cookie sheet with button cookies—add lots of character.

Materials For Basic Doll:
patterns begin on page 128
¼ yard each of 6 Christmas miniprint
  fabrics
white and black felt
muslin
white thread
polyester stuffing
½ yard (½″-wide) white cluny lace
water-soluble fabric marker
fine-line permanent markers
  (black, red)
pink colored pencil (for cheeks)

Note: ¼″ seam allowance is included in all pattern pieces, and all seams are ¼″ unless otherwise instructed.

BASIC DOLL: Cut out all pattern pieces as indicated.

Appliqué face piece to body, using narrow satin stitch. (For Kris only, from black felt, cut belt and appliqué to body front.)

Fold arm piece in half, right sides facing, and stitch down edge opposite fold. Turn right side out. Repeat for remaining arm. Pin arms to right side of body front, with seam down and raw edges aligned. Pin body pieces with right sides facing and stitch around body, leaving an opening at bottom as indicated.

Stitch legs, right sides together, leaving top edge open. Turn right side out and stuff firmly. Stuff body and insert leg tops in opening. Folding raw edges under, hand-stitch body closed, securing legs.

From white felt, cut 4 hands per doll. Using white thread, overcast-stitch around hands, leaving open where indicated. Lightly stuff hands. Stuff arms and turn

raw edges under ⅛″. Insert hands, with thumbs facing up, and stitch to wrists. For Mrs. Kringle, stitch cluny lace to wrists while hemming. Pull threads tightly, gathering ends of arms and lace to form cuffs.

Draw face, using water-soluble marker. (To erase mistakes, dampen face till ink disappears and let dry completely; then draw again.) Trace over markings with permanent markers (colors indicated). Lightly shade cheeks with pink colored pencil.

Materials for Kris Kringle:
⅛ yard red velour knit
10″ (⅜-wide) green print ribbon
hot-glue gun and glue sticks
scraps of green felt
1 (¼″) jingle bell
6″ (¼″-wide) white rabbit-fur strip (or
  white fleece)
1 small red bead
1 (½″) red heart button
Pingouin "Intrigue" white yarn

Note: Pingouin white yarn gives beard a special texture with the silk threads woven into the mohair. (Mohair can be substituted, but is not quite as fluffy.)

Fold red velour in half, right sides facing, and transfer pattern for cap. Stitch, leaving bottom open. Cut out cap, adding ⅛″ seam allowance, and turn right side out. Lightly stuff hat, turn raw edges under ⅛″, and blindstitch to head.

Tie green ribbon into a bow and tack bow and bell to end of cap. Starting at center back of cap, glue fur trim around bottom edge of cap, overlapping ends slightly. From green felt, cut 2 holly leaves; glue red bead and leaves to cap. Tack heart button to center of belt. For eyebrow, wrap yarn around pinky finger twice. Stitch center above eye and fluff yarn. Repeat for other eyebrow.

For beard and hair, wrap yarn around index finger 3 times. Tack center to face, starting at right side just below cap. Continue making and tacking loops, working down and around face and up over eyes again. Trim and shape beard.

Materials for Mrs. Kringle:
cluny lace (remainder from basic doll)
1 (⅜″) red heart button
miniprint (from basic doll)
½ yard (¾″-wide) gathered eyelet lace
¼ yard (⅝″-wide) red/green plaid ribbon
white mohair yarn
2½″ square piece of cardboard
2 (¼″) red beads
4″ (⅛″-wide) red satin ribbon
hot-glue gun and glue sticks
2 reindeer shank buttons
1 (2″ x 2½″) piece of tin
hole punch
12″ (¼″-wide) red satin ribbon

Using remainder of cluny lace, turn ends under, gather lace, and tack along face edge to form collar. Tack heart button 1″ below face edge at center of body.

For skirt, cut a 2¼″ x 18″ rectangle from fabric. Turn one long edge under ¼″ and stitch eyelet lace to folded hem. With right sides facing, stitch 2¼″ ends together. Sew a row of gathering stitches ⅛″ from raw edge of skirt piece (leaving needle connected) and slip skirt onto doll. Position skirt just under the arms, seam centered at the back of doll; pull gathers to fit doll and knot thread. Adjust gathers evenly around body and tack in place. Overlap one long edge of plaid ribbon over raw edge of skirt; tie bow at back. Tack ribbon edge to skirt.

For hair, wrap yarn loosely around one edge of cardboard 25 times. Slip looped yarn off, and tie a piece of yarn around middle of loops to form "center part." Tack "center part" to upper forehead, twist sides slightly and tack bottom of loops to sides of face edge. (See Diagram.) Sew red beads just under hairline for earrings. Loop another length of yarn 25 times around cardboard. Slip loops off, tie a piece of yarn through one end, and knot. Repeat for opposite end and clip tie ends. Tack one knotted end to back of head, behind earring. Twist yarn 3 times and attach remaining knotted end to other side, behind opposite earring. Arrange yarn to meet at top of head and cover evenly. Tie (⅛″-wide) ribbon into a bow and glue to top of head.

Using sharp scissors, cut off backs of reindeer buttons. Set aside. For cookie sheet, using a hole punch, make a hole at each 2″ end of tin. Using threaded needle, attach cookie sheet to hands, sewing back and forth through hole to hand several times, for each hand. Cut (¼″-wide) ribbon in half and tie 2 bows; glue on top of threads securing hands to cookie sheet. Glue reindeer buttons to cookie sheet.

Diagram—Making Hair

Center Part

Twist and tack looped pieces to sides.

Storybook Bear: A Keepsake Ornament

At times, an artist's rendition of an animal embodies such a lifelike quality and endearing personality that it steals your heart. We think this dignified little bear, a sure-to-be heirloom ornament, is one of those designs. You can create your own storybook bear, stunning in Victorian finery, with these simple instructions. Just don't be surprised when she reveals her own lovable, one-of-a-kind personality.

Materials:
patterns begin on page 128
1 small package Sculpey III modeling
  compound in off-white
long straight pins
acrylic paints (tan, black)
fine paintbrush
⅛ yard unbleached muslin
polyester stuffing
⅛ yard burgundy moiré fabric
⅜ yard each of 2 kinds of (¼″-wide)
  ivory flat lace trims
¼ yard (1¼″-wide) ivory embroidered
  lace trim
1 small burgundy silk flower
scrap of (⅛″-wide) green satin ribbon
miniature book (preferably about
  bears)
hot-glue gun and glue sticks

For head, using 3 sticks of Sculpey, work compound with hands until soft and pliable; roll into a ball. For shoulders, using 2 sticks of compound, roll into a ball. Position the small ball under the large one and stick a long straight pin into bottom center of small ball, pushing through to large ball, anchoring head on shoulders.

For snout, use one stick of compound and work it into an oval. Gently mold oval into front of face. For each ear, using ¼ of a stick, make an oval ball. Position at top back of head for ear. Gently mold oval to curve around toward the front of the face. Repeat for the other ear.

For nose, roll a small amount of compound into a tiny ball and place at end of snout. Using a long pin, lightly score face, scoring away from snout outwards toward side of face and ears. Make vertical score lines on back of head from neck to top of head. For eye sockets, make ⅛″ indentations with tip of handle of fine paintbrush.

For each arm, using ½ stick of compound, work compound with hands until pliable; mold into a long oval, indent for wrist, and mold a small paw, slightly curving paw inward. Lightly score paw from wrist outward with pin. Following the man-

ufacturer's instructions, bake all the sculpted pieces, to harden.

Using diluted tan paint, stain head and paws. Let dry for 5 minutes and blot. Paint nose, mouth, eyes, and eyelashes black, referring to photograph as a guide. Let sculpted pieces dry overnight.

Fold muslin fabric in half, right sides facing, and transfer body pattern to fabric. (Do not cut out.) Machine-stitch body on outline, leaving open as indicated on pattern. Adding ¼″ seam allowance, cut out body, and clip corners and curves. Turn and stuff body firmly. Insert shoulder piece into neck of body. Turn neckline of body under ⅛″ and gather around neck of clay. Insert arm ends of paws into ends of fabric arms. Turn fabric under ⅛″ and gather tightly around clay arm at wrist. Repeat for other arm. Using diluted tan paint, stain bottom portion of muslin legs.

For dress, transfer pattern to burgundy fabric and cut out 2 dress pieces. Using ⅛″ seam allowance, machine-stitch shoulder and underarm/side seams; clip curves, turn, and press. Turn neckline under ⅛″ and make small gathering stitches around neckline. Do not clip thread; put dress on bear. Pull thread tightly and gather around neck; knot and clip thread. Turn sleeve edges under ⅛″, gather around sleeves as for neckline, and pull thread tightly around wrists; knot and clip thread. Glue scalloped lace trim around sleeves for cuffs. Hand-stitch short ends of 1¼″ lace together and place around neck for collar. Turn raw edge under ⅛″ and make small gathering stitches around edge; pull thread tightly to gather collar around neck; knot and clip thread. Glue silk flower to left side of collar at neckline.

Cut small lace rosette from lace trim and glue to right ear. Tie ribbon in a bow and glue to center of rosette.

Turn hem of dress under ¼″ and hand-stitch lace trim to hem of dress. Hand-stitch a row of lace around dress ½″ above hem. Glue the small book to the left hand of the bear.

HANDMADE WITH LOVE

Greet this chapter like an old friend—one whose creative skills you have always admired. Because within these pages is a collection of the brightest, cleverest, most up-to-date designs around. And since Christmas lists never get any shorter, get started now, to create gifts that reflect love, thoughtfulness, caring, and of course—you.

Christmas Eve Nightie

Start a new tradition—let this be the one gift to open Christmas Eve so that your little miss will be appropriately dressed when morning comes. Appliquéd apples in a tree formation are supported by a whimsical gift-box "trunk," and bows and ruffles add the feminine touch.

Materials:
patterns begin on page 128
green nightshirt
⅓ yard lightweight iron-on interfacing
½ yard (36″-wide) red pindot
scraps of brown pindot, green mini-plaid, and Christmas miniprint
thread (red, green, brown, white)
1 yard (¾″-wide) striped ribbon
1 red apple button

Note: Nightshirt patterns are available. If you make a nightshirt instead of using a purchased one, complete all the appliqué before final assembly and add the ruffle to finish the hem.

Fuse interfacing to the back of all appliqué fabrics. (*Note:* Cut apples from one end of red pindot fabric leaving the remainder for the ruffle.) Cut 12 apples from red pindot, 12 stems from brown pindot, 12 leaves from green miniplaid, and 1 tree trunk from Christmas miniprint.

Fuse an 11″ x 13″ piece of interfacing to the inside center front of the nightshirt. With nightshirt front right side up, arrange 4 rows of apples on center (area backed by the interfacing). Follow photograph for placement of apples, being sure to leave about 1″ between rows of apples for the stems and leaves. Center the tree trunk about 1″ below the last row of apples. Arrange a stem and leaf for each apple. Pin appliqué pieces to secure.

Fuse interfacing inside the right sleeve near the cuff and pin an apple, stem, and leaf in place on the outside of the sleeve. Fuse interfacing inside the left sleeve near the shoulder and pin an apple, stem, and leaf in place as before.

With matching thread, machine-appliqué all pieces. To add highlights to apples, satin-stitch a ¼″ curved white line (see photograph).

Stitch a 1½″ length of striped ribbon to the middle of the trunk. Tie a 12″ length of the ribbon in a bow. Tack bow to top of trunk piece.

Use remaining striped ribbon to make a 6-loop bow. Tack bow at neck edge. Sew apple button to center of bow.

To determine length of ruffle, measure around the bottom hem of nightshirt, double the measurement, and add 2″. Cut 4″-wide strips of red pindot fabric to equal ruffle length. Stitch strips together to make a continuous length of fabric. Fold fabric in half lengthwise, wrong sides facing, and gather to fit hem of nightshirt. With raw edges aligned and right sides facing, pin ruffle to nightshirt, adjusting gathers evenly. Stitch with a ¼″ seam. On right side of nightshirt, topstitch a green wavy line above the ruffle, and through the seam allowances.

Swiss-Style
Baby Bunting

This Christmas, keep the baby on your list snug in a colorful, puffy baby bunting. It's decorated with a motif taken from the quaint village of Zermatt, which lies in the shadow of the Matterhorn in Switzerland. Cozily enfolded in this happy scene, Baby will coo with contentment. The details on the mother and child are painted, but if you're handier with a needle than a brush, you could easily embroider them.

This bunting does double duty. Zip the Velcro, button up the sides, cinch the bottom, and Baby is warm and safely portable. Then, at home, unfasten the bunting and use it as a cover to tuck Baby in for a warm winter's nap.

Materials:
patterns, diagrams begin on page 128
1⅛ yards (45″-wide) bleached muslin
water-soluble fabric marker
⅛ yard (45″-wide) green fabric
4″ square of blue fabric
⅛ yard (45″-wide) brown print fabric
scrap of pink fabric
¼ yard (45″-wide) double-sided fusible
  web fabric
thread to match all fabrics
black and red acrylic paints
small round paintbrush
¾ yard (45″-wide) red fabric
4⅛ yards (½″-wide) plaid piping
1 yard (45″-wide) batting
23″ (¾″-wide) Velcro

Cut a strip of muslin 7½″ x 43″. Following Diagram, transfer patterns for trees, mother, and baby in sled to strip. Cut appliqué pieces from fabrics as indicated on pattern. Cut matching pieces from fusible web fabric. Fuse appliqué pieces to muslin, following manufacturer's instructions.

Using matching thread, machine-appliqué pieces in place. Stitch into appliqués for details as indicated by lines on patterns.

With water-soluble marker, transfer facial and clothing details to mother and baby. Following pattern, paint with acrylic paints.

Cut 1 (9″ x 43″) and 1 (16½″ x 43″) rectangle from red fabric. Align 43″ edge of smaller rectangle with top edge of design piece, right sides facing. Use a ½″ seam to sew together. Repeat to sew other rectangle to bottom of design. Press seams toward red fabric.

Cut 5 (5″) lengths of piping. Loop in half and pin to right edge of bunting, raw edges aligned and loops to inside front. Position end loops 2″ from corners, with 3 remaining loops evenly spaced between them. Machine-baste in place. Pull plaid fabric away from cording at seam allowance and trim excess cording.

For piping buttons, cut 5 (13½″) lengths of piping. Tie 3 knots in center of each length. Machine-baste buttons, raw edges

aligned, to side opposite loops, spacing to line up with loops.

Cut 1 (31″ x 43″) piece from muslin (for backing) and 1 same-size piece from batting. Baste together ⅜″ from sides and top and 1½″ from bottom.

Separate Velcro and sew 1 strip along right side and 1 along left side of bunting backing, ⅝″ from side edges.

Right sides facing, pin bunting front to backing. Using a ½″ seam, sew together along top and side edges. Trim corners, trim batting in seam allowances, and turn to right side through bottom.

For bottom casing, with fabric marker, draw a line parallel to and 1½″ from raw edge. Stitch along this line. Trim batting from casing area. Press raw edges of fabric ½″ to inside, and with a ¼″ seam, sew together. Sew a second seam ⅛″ from edge.

With red thread, machine-quilt on red fabric ⅛″ from edges of design piece along both sides. Working from these lines, use fabric marker to draw a 2″ grid over entire surface of both red fabric pieces. Holding fabric taut, machine-quilt along those lines. Change to white thread, and machine-quilt around appliqués.

Transfer heart pattern to muslin and fusible web fabric 6 times each and cut out. Button together sides of bunting and center 3 hearts on each side below design, placing along third row of quilted squares below panel. See photo. Unbutton bunting. Fuse hearts to bunting, following manufacturer's instructions. With white thread, machine-appliqué around hearts.

Cut 1½ yards of piping and insert in casing. Tie a double knot 1½″ from each end. Pull back plaid fabric and cut away ½″ of cording. Fold plaid fabric to inside and blindstitch to finish ends.

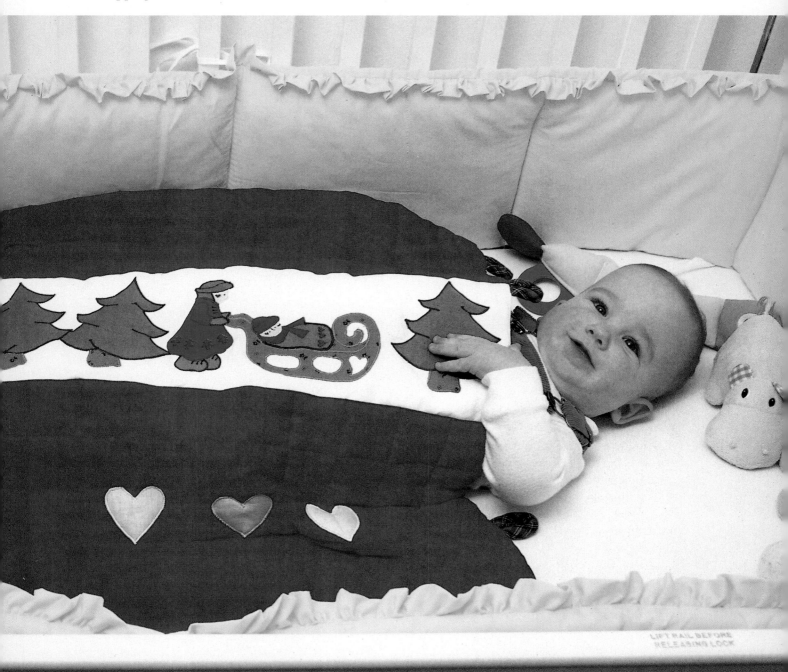

Clowning Around

Set the stage for a cheery holiday with this group of happy clowns. Colorful and sprightly, with arms and legs outstretched, each clown seems to be dancing a jig. Made from scraps of various print fabrics, the lively lot can be whipped up with little time and expense.

Use the clowns on the tree as an alternative to Christmas balls or ribbons. Or make some for package toppers. Or attach several in a continuous clown circle to slip around a basket as shown here.

Materials (for one clown):
patterns begin on page 128
10″ square cotton print (for arms and
  legs)
stuffing
2″ x 4″ piece of muslin (for head)
3″ x 8″ piece of cotton print (for hat)
thread to match
embroidery floss (black, dark red)
2 small black beads
blush
cotton swab
¼ yard (1″-wide) pregathered lace
¼ yard narrow jute cording
craft glue
1 small bell

Transfer arm and leg patterns and markings to cotton print fabric and cut out (see Diagram for layout).

Fold fabric for arms in half, long edges together, with right sides facing. Stitch long edges with a ¼″ seam. Turn. Fold fabric at open ends under ¼″ and press. Sew a running stitch ⅛″ from one folded edge. Pull thread to gather, close end, and tie off. Stuff arms loosely. Gather other end and close as above. Repeat procedure for legs.

Place legs on flat surface, seam side down. Place arms next to legs, with seam side down. Wrap thread tightly several times around center of arm and leg piece to form body.

Transfer pattern for head to muslin twice and cut out. Transfer markings for face to 1 head piece (front). Transfer hat pattern and markings to print fabric and cut out 2 (1 reversed). Position one hat piece on face front with dots aligned. Fold hat edge under ¼″ and blindstitch to face piece. In the same manner, stitch together hat back and back of head. With right sides facing and head-hat seams aligned, stitch pieces together leaving no opening. Cut a small slit in the back of the head to turn. (Be sure that tip of hat is completely turned.) Stuff hat and head firmly, keeping the shape flat. Whipstitch slit closed.

With one strand black floss, embroider eyelashes, using straight stitches. With black floss, sew black beads in place for eyes. With one strand dark red floss, embroider mouth, using outline stitch. With cotton swab, apply a small amount of blush to cheeks.

Make a running stitch along pregathered edge of lace and pull to form a circle. With chin at center of lace circle, whipstitch lace to back of head. Sew lace and head to body. Tie a bow in jute and knot ends. Glue below clown's chin. Sew small bell to the tip of hat.

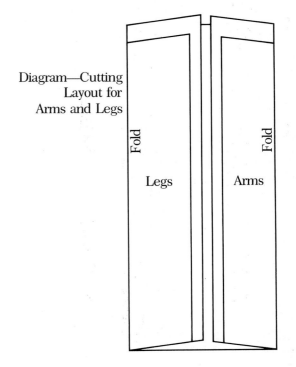

Diagram—Cutting
Layout for
Arms and Legs

Fold   Legs   Arms   Fold

Wearable Art

Give big, roomy sweatshirts a seasonal appeal with an imaginative dose of painting and stenciling. Rows of trees, checkerboards, and hearts are stenciled on the bright white shirt. On the green shirt, an abstract tree is outlined in paint, and flourishes of color are added with painted shrink-art ornaments.

PAINTED SWEATSHIRT
Materials:
patterns begin on page 128
white sweatshirt
¾"-wide masking tape
kitchen sponge
acrylic paints: red, green, brown
textile medium
¾"-wide flat shader brush

Wash shirt and dry in a hot dryer. Place a smooth, waterproof surface inside shirt to prevent paint from bleeding through.

Note: For all painting, mix 1 part paint with 1 part textile medium.

To make checkerboard band, apply 7 strips of tape, edge to edge, horizontally across lower front of shirt. Remove second, fourth, and sixth strips. Then apply more tape strips vertically, laying them edge to edge and covering horizontal strips. Remove every other strip. Run thumbnail along edges of tape to secure, so that paint won't bleed under tape.

Cut three 1"-square pieces from sponge. Dip one piece into red paint mixture; blot several times on paper towel. When much of the paint is removed, dab sponge on squares blocked by tape. Allow to dry. Remove tape.

Apply 5 strips of tape horizontally over the checkerboard area, carefully aligning tape over painted squares. Remove the second and fourth strips. Apply more strips vertically, edge to edge, covering horizontal strips. Remove every other strip, leaving painted squares covered. Repeat painting procedure. Allow to dry; remove tape.

For red checkerboard around neck and above cuffs, paint freehand, using ¾" paintbrush. Paint squares the width of the brush and use paint sparingly.

Transfer tree and stand pattern onto shirt, spacing trees evenly and referring to photograph for placement. (Five trees were painted on this large shirt.) Paint trees green, using sponge technique, and using corner of sponge to paint branch details. Sponge-paint bases brown.

Make each heart in neckline checkerboard by dipping the tip of a pencil eraser or a blunt-end paintbrush handle in red paint and making 2 dots in an unpainted square. Pull the paint down from the dots to form the point of the heart. Paint one or a small cluster of hearts on one or both sleeves, if desired.

Allow shirt to dry overnight. To set paint, place plain brown paper or paper toweling inside shirt and over painted areas. Press with cool iron.

SHRINK-ART SWEATSHIRT
Materials:
patterns begin on page 128
green sweatshirt
white chalk
acrylic paints (white, red, blue, black,
  antique gold, dark green)
shrink-art plastic in transparent and
  opaque
paintbrushes: #2, #1 liner, #3 round
round toothpicks
⅛" hole punch
needle and thread

Wash shirt and dry in hot dryer. Place smooth, waterproof surface inside shirt to prevent paint from bleeding through.

Using chalk, draw tree freehand onto front of shirt, referring to photograph for placement. Squeeze white paint from tube or bottle onto shirt, following chalk lines, but keeping painted lines loose and swirling. Let dry overnight. Cut out ornament shapes from shrink-art plastic.

You can paint on the back of transparent

shrink-art plastic, leaving front clear and glassy, or paint on the front for a slightly textured effect. If front of ornament is to be painted, paint background first; let dry; then paint details. If back of ornament is to be painted, paint details first; let dry; then paint background. Paint details of reverse-painted ornament by placing ornament over pattern and tracing with paint.

To shade ornament, paint a solid color and, while paint is still wet, blend in black along one edge and white along the other. Add a white highlight.

To paint tiny hearts, apply 2 dots of paint for each and, using a toothpick, pull paint down to form the point of the heart.

Allow shapes to dry overnight; punch 2 holes at top of each, following pattern. Follow manufacturer's instructions to shrink. Sew ornaments onto shirt.

A Mug for Dad

If Dad has all the ties and socks a man could want, maybe he'd get a kick out of a more personal gift. A mug, boldly painted with a tree and "Dad," will put him in a festive mood. Even little hands can execute the details on this mug (under the supervision of an adult), and a short turn in the oven renders it dishwasher-safe.

In fact, this gift's so quick and easy, you might want to add a "Grand" and make another very special man happy on Christmas morning.

Materials:
red ceramic coffee mug
dish detergent
ammonia
soft-lead pencil
white model paint
small paintbrush

Mix small amounts of detergent and ammonia in a large bowl of water. Soak the mug in this mixture for 15 minutes. Remove the mug from the bowl, being careful not to touch the area to be painted, and rinse under hot water. Let dry.

Sketch a tree shape on paper and cut out. Lightly trace the pattern outline onto the mug with the pencil (see photograph for placement).

Lay mug on its side. Shake the paint well. Dip wooden end of paintbrush into paint and, following the tree outline, drop dots of paint onto mug. Complete the tree outline first; then fill in with dots.

Lightly sketch the name below the tree. Paint the outlines and place large dots at beginnings and ends of letters.

Let paint dry for 48 hours. To dishwasher-proof the mug, place it in a 210° oven for 15 minutes. Be sure to keep the area well-ventilated.

Christmas Sweatshirt With Celestial Charm

Your favorite little cherub will be charmed—as will her daddy—by a celestial cross-stitched sweatshirt. The angelic design, worked simply on waste-canvas, makes a sturdy sweatshirt as sweet as it is practical.

Materials:
charts begin on page 128
5″ x 7″ piece (8.5-count) waste canvas
child-size white sweatshirt
masking tape
embroidery floss (see color key)
#24 tapestry needle
tweezers

Position canvas 2″ below center neck edge of sweatshirt. Tape in place. Cross-stitch the design, following the chart and color key, stitching over the canvas and through the sweatshirt with 4 strands of floss. (To keep the stitches even, be sure the outer point of each cross is in the center of the appropriate hole in the canvas.)

Backstitch areas indicated by dark lines on chart with 2 strands of black floss. Backstitch words with 3 strands of Christmas-red floss. Make French knot eyes with 2 strands of blue-green floss, wrapped once around the needle.

When stitching is complete, remove masking tape. Thoroughly wet the waste canvas with cold water. Using tweezers, pull the individual threads of the canvas to remove. Allow garment to dry.

This Big Puppy Is a Cuddle-Buddy

Lickety-split, you can whip together this cuddle-buddy for a little boy or girl. Big Puppy wears a child's size-three clothes and is tolerant of all kinds of attire. Give him a vest, holster, and hat, and your little sheriff has a deputy. Then, when playtime is over, he'll gladly don a nightcap and nightshirt and drift off to sleep with his favorite playmate.

To keep the pals safe, make sure you choose a flame-retardant fabric and stuffing. If you're making the puppy for a toddler, you might substitute embroidered or fabric facial details for plastic ones that could be pulled off and swallowed.

Materials:
patterns begin on page 128
1½ yards (45″-wide) light brown fake fur
13″ x 17″ piece of dark brown fake fur (for ears and tail)
13″ x 11″ piece of light brown fabric (to line ears)
heavy-duty thread to match
stuffing
2 (2½ mm) brown plastic eyes
1 (3 mm) brown plastic nose
hot-glue gun and glue sticks

From light brown fur, cut out 4 arms (2 reversed), 4 bodies (2 reversed), 2 heads (1 reversed), and 1 muzzle piece. From dark brown fur, cut out 2 ears and 1 tail. From lining cut out 2 ears.

Note: All seams are ½″. Backstitch at beginning and end of every seam to secure.

Fold tail in half lengthwise with right sides facing. Leaving straight edge open, stitch tail and turn.

Mark arm and body pieces, front and back, right and left. Position front arm pieces on front body pieces where indicated on pattern, with right sides facing and raw edges aligned, and stitch together. Repeat to attach back arm pieces to back body pieces. Place both front pieces together, right sides facing and raw edges aligned. Stitch together along center seam. Place each back half along front piece, right sides facing and raw edges aligned and stitch along side seams, leaving back center and neck seams open.

On back center seam, position straight edge of tail as indicated on pattern, tail to inside and raw edges aligned. Stitch center back seam, leaving open between Xs, as indicated on the pattern, for turning and stuffing.

Place 1 ear lining and 1 fur ear piece together, right sides facing, and stitch, leaving straight edge open. Turn. Repeat for other ear.

Cut slits for ears on each side of head, as indicated on pattern. Stitch darts at top of head and neck. Insert raw edge of ears ¾″ into slits, making sure right sides are facing, lining side is to bottom, and raw edges are aligned.

On wrong side of head, stitch slit closed, securing ear. With right sides of head pieces facing and making sure ears are free, stitch from nose to top of head and around back of head to neck.

Pin muzzle in place, right sides facing. Starting at neck on one side and ending at other side, stitch muzzle to head. Turn head right side out.

To furrow puppy's brow, follow lines on pattern, and handstitch through head, sewing from the front line to the back line, and then back to front. Pull all stitches tightly. Stitch through several times and secure thread.

Insert head into body, right sides facing, and stitch together along neck. Turn puppy through remaining opening. To stuff, use small amounts of stuffing at a time and work it into arms and legs with a stick or dowel. Stuff puppy lightly where arms and legs meet body (so that limbs can bend). Stuff remainder of body firmly. Blindstitch back opening closed.

Glue eyes and nose in place.

Nordic-Inspired Design

After a glorious day spent on the slopes—or in search of that perfect Christmas tree—put on this good-looking Nordic-design sweater and cozy up to a roaring fire with your family and friends. A handsome wooden tray and coasters emblazoned with the same reindeer-and-spruce pattern hold warming cups of cocoa and Yuletide cheer.

The Nordic design, worked in duplicate stitch on a purchased or hand-knit sweater, can be translated to any size and is a gift that any member of your family would love to don for après-ski relaxation or casual holiday festivities.

The wooden tray and coasters, especially handy for holiday spur-of-the-moment entertaining, make thoughtful hostess gifts. And the coasters that complement the tray can easily become ornaments for the tree.

NORDIC SWEATER
Materials:
charts, diagrams begin on page 128
sweater
tapestry needle
yarn similar in weight to that of sweater: green, red, black, white

Size of design will vary according to gauge of sweater used: if the sweater has more than 6 stitches to the inch, the design will be smaller; if fewer, the design will be larger. To determine gauge, lay sweater on a flat surface, and using a ruler, count the number of stitches knit in one horizontal inch. The design is approximately 22″ x 6⅝″ on a sweater with 6 stitches to the inch.

Fold sweater in half lengthwise and baste along fold to mark center front. Decide on position of design on sweater and, following chart, stitch tree first. To duplicate-stitch, starting from wrong side of sweater, pull needle up through the stitch below the first stitch to be covered, leaving about a 4″ tail of yarn. Pass the needle under stitch above the one to be covered.

Reinsert the needle into the stitch through which you started. Repeat, working from left to right, covering knit stitches with embroidery stitches (see Diagram). Pull stitches carefully so that embroidery completely covers knitted stitches without altering tension.

Using tree as reference point, stitch reindeer and diamonds. Then stitch horizontal diamond bands. To secure end of yarn, weave end through several stitches on the back of the sweater.

TRAY AND COASTERS
Materials:
patterns begin on page 128
**1 rectangular basswood plaque with an
    11″ x 14″ flat surface (for tray)**
    ***Note:* Light-colored, fine-grained
    pine without knots may be used.**
**1 (3¼″) light-colored wood disk (for
    each coaster/ornament)**
sandpaper
**drill with ¹⁄₁₆″ bit and bit to match
    screw size**
scrap of lightweight cardboard
11″ x 14″ tracing paper
**11″ x 14″ graphite paper (do not use
    carbon paper)**
stylus
masking tape
**wood-burning pen with interchange-
    able points**
**universal or all-purpose point for
    wood-burning pen**
black carpet thread
2 (4⅞″) satin brass drawer pulls
coarse steel wool
kneaded-rubber eraser
light-colored stain
satin varnish

Lightly sand plaque and disks in direction of wood grain. For ornaments, drill
a hole ³⁄₁₆″ from disk's center top edge.

Out of lightweight cardboard, cut a ⅜″-
square template for diamond shape in the
pattern. Transfer tray pattern onto tracing
paper, using a straightedge for straight
lines and template for diamond shapes. For
coasters and ornaments, trace only the
reindeer shape onto tracing paper.

With graphite paper between each pattern and the wood, center patterns, positioning reindeer in center of disk and tray
pattern squarely on the plaque. Secure
papers with masking tape. With stylus,
transfer patterns to wood, again using
straightedge and template as guides.

Remove paper from wood. Practice using
the wood-burning pen on wood scraps before you begin. Remember, once a mark

has been burned, it cannot be removed, so
work carefully. If pen becomes caked with
charred wood, clean it by rubbing the hot
point over steel wool.

Following the manufacturer's instructions, carefully and evenly trace with the
wood-burning pen the marked pattern on
the wood. Erase graphite marks from wood
surfaces. Stain plaque and disks; let dry.
Varnish all surfaces.

Attach drawer pulls at centers of short
edges of plaque. Run desired length of
thread through hole of each ornament and
knot.

Roses and Bows

Beautiful and practical, this embroidered pastel needle case will end the mad search for needles and pins. A double layer of lacy edging peeks from between the softly padded hearts, and a satin ribbon tie holds them together. Inside are blue chintz fabric and ribbons placed on the diagonal to hold sewing sundries securely.

Materials:
patterns and charts begin on page 128
¼ yard (36″-wide) light blue miniprint
embroidery floss (see color key)
embroidery hoop
12″ square of mat board
6″ x 12″ piece of craft fleece
¼ yard (36″-wide) medium blue solid
  chintz fabric
craft glue
½ yard (¼″-wide) flat white lace trim
1 yard (⅝″-wide) pleated white lace
  trim
¾ yard (⅜″-wide) white satin ribbon
⅓ yard (1″-wide) blue grosgrain ribbon

Cut an 8″ square from the light blue miniprint. Transfer the embroidery design to the center of the 8″ square of fabric. Center square in hoop and work design, using 4 strands of floss. Block embroidered piece.

Transfer heart pattern to mat board 4 times and cut out. Use mat board heart as a guide and cut out 2 fleece pieces. Cut out 2 hearts from blue chintz and 1 from miniprint. Center embroidered design on pattern and cut out.

Place embroidered heart face down and center 1 fleece heart and 1 mat board heart on top. Clip curves, fold edges over mat board, and glue. Glue ¼″ trim around back edge of heart. Glue ⅝″ trim behind ¼″ trim around heart. Place miniprint heart right side down and center fleece and mat board on top as above. Clip, glue fabric to back of heart, and glue pleated lace around edge.

Place embroidered heart on the left and miniprint heart on the right, side by side, wrong sides up, about ¼″ apart. Lay white satin ribbon across the middle of both hearts, with free ends extending about 8½″ on each side, and glue ribbon to hearts. (See Diagram.)

Glue chintz hearts to remaining mat board hearts as above, omitting the fleece and trim. Cut blue grosgrain ribbon in half. Place ribbon diagonally across chintz hearts as shown in photograph. Glue ribbon ends to backs of hearts. Glue chintz hearts to design heart and miniprint heart. Tie satin ribbon in a bow.

Diagram—Attaching Ribbon Ties
Glue ribbon in place to join hearts.

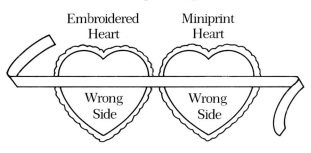

91

Potpourri and Paper: A Cross-Stitch Sachet

A delicate rose, cross-stitched on perforated paper, gives a hint of the delicious scent this sachet emits. It's quick to assemble and has many uses—tie it to the top of a package, hang it from a tree, and when the season is past, let its perfume permeate a closet or drawer.

A plus is that when the potpourri has lost its power, you can simply untie the ribbon, replace the mixture, and the sachet will continue to delight the senses.

Materials:
charts begin on page 128
8″ square of perforated paper
embroidery floss (see color key)
pinking shears
craft knife
4¼″ square of perforated paper
¾ yard (¼″-wide) ribbon
⅛ cup potpourri

Stitch design on 8″ square of perforated paper following chart. With pinking shears, trim paper on all sides, 3 holes from the stitchery.

Follow chart and use craft knife to cut away a slot of paper 2 holes wide and 4 high. Count 4 holes to the right and cut out another slot the same size. Following chart, cut out slots around design.

With pinking shears, trim all edges of 4¼″ square of paper for back of sachet. Center front piece on back and use as guide to mark cuts for back. Cut away corresponding slots of paper.

Use slots to align front and back pieces. Beginning at top left corner, leaving 9″ of ribbon free, weave ribbon through slots to top right-hand corner. Carefully insert potpourri in top of sachet. Weave the remaining ends of ribbon to center and tie in a bow to close sachet.

A Handy Mitt

Lend the Christmas baker a hand with this quilted and appliquéd hot mitt. Simple graphic shapes on a red-checked background pronounce the season loud and clear. Cushy and thick, this hot mitt will help safeguard your favorite cook.

Materials:
patterns begin on page 128
⅓ yard (36″-wide) red checked fabric (for mitt)
⅓ yard (36″-wide) red print fabric (for lining and hearts)
⅓ yard batting
scrap of green print fabric (for trees and triangles)
scrap of white fabric (for background)
thread to match fabrics
glue stick
paper
12″ piece precovered white piping
4″ piece (½″-wide) red ribbon

Note: All seam allowances are ⅛″ unless otherwise indicated.

Transfer mitt pattern to red-checked fabric and cut 2. Do same with red print fabric and batting. Transfer heart pattern to red print fabric and cut 3. Transfer triangle pattern to green fabric and cut 2. Transfer tree pattern to green fabric and cut 3. Cut a 3″ square from the white fabric for the design background.

Using photograph for placement, lay triangles on white square. Turn edges of triangles under ⅛″ and stitch to square. Glue block to mitt front. Glue one heart to tip of thumb; glue trees and remaining hearts in alternating pattern along straight edge of mitt.

Place a piece of paper under the mitt front and pin to secure. Machine-appliqué around white block, hearts, and trees. Remove paper.

Pin one batting piece under mitt front; hand-quilt around triangles, hearts, and trees. With right sides facing, layer mitt back on mitt front with remaining batting piece on top. Pin all layers together. Leaving straight edge open, stitch around mitt. Trim batting in seam allowances and turn.

Pin piping and straight edge of mitt with right sides facing and raw edges aligned, and stitch piping to mitt. Turn raw edges of piping to wrong side of mitt. With corded edge showing on right side of mitt, iron. Place lining pieces with right sides facing and, leaving straight edge open, stitch around edge. Do not turn. Turn fabric under ¼″ along straight edge and iron. Sew ribbon loop to straight edge of mitt, centering loop on seam above thumb.

Slip the lining into the mitt. Whipstitch piping on mitt to lining.

YOUR CHRISTMAS KITCHEN

Many generations of jubilant cooks have laid sumptuous Christmas dinners before their families. In this chapter, we summon that culinary heritage, with recipes based on the glowing descriptions of food in Dickens's *A Christmas Carol.* In addition to those delicious dishes, you'll find splendid concoctions for entertaining, gift-giving—every part of your celebrations.

A Christmas Carol:
Holiday Selections from Dickens

Conjure classic images of Christmas in your mind. Chances are, much of what you cherish about the season you owe to Charles Dickens. In *A Christmas Carol,* written nearly 150 years ago, Dickens captured the timeless richness of Victorian Christmases, and with the dishes presented here, we pay homage to the great writer who described so well the depth of the holiday spirit and the joy of its accompanying celebration. Enjoy morsels of his treasured text as you peruse these recipes for classics such as Creamy Eggnog Punch, Goose with Sage and Onion, Sweet Chestnut Soufflé, Marvelous Mincemeat Pie, and Flaming Brandy Plum Pudding.

CREAMY EGGNOG PUNCH

12 eggs, separated
1 (16-ounce) package powdered
  sugar, sifted
1 cup light rum
1 cup bourbon
1 quart half-and-half
1 quart whipping cream
Freshly grated nutmeg (optional)

Beat egg yolks in a large bowl at high speed of an electric mixer until foamy. Gradually add powdered sugar, beating until thick and lemon colored. Stir in light rum and bourbon. Cover and refrigerate 1 hour. Add half-and-half and whipping cream, stirring well; pour mixture into a large punch bowl.

Beat egg whites (at room temperature) until soft peaks form. Gently fold 2 cups yolk mixture into egg whites; then fold egg whites into remaining yolk mixture in punch bowl. Cover and refrigerate eggnog until thoroughly chilled. Sprinkle with grated nutmeg just before serving, if desired. Yield: about 4 quarts.

*H*eaped up on the floor, to form a kind of throne, were tur-keys, geese, game, poultry, brawn, great joints of meat, sucking-pigs, long wreaths of sausages, mince-pies, plum-puddings, barrels of oysters, red-hot chestnuts, cherry-cheeked apples, juicy oranges, luscious pears, immense twelfth-cakes, and seething bowls of punch, that made the chamber dim with their delicious steam. In easy state upon this couch, there sat a jolly Giant, glorious to see; who bore a glowing torch, in shape not unlike Plenty's horn.

Opposite: When you put out the sandwich platter this year, let marinated beef tenderloin gather appreciative murmurs. Flavored by port, brandy, herbs, and spices, this dish may inspire a literary tribute all its own.

BEEF TENDERLOIN
PARTY SANDWICHES

½ cup port wine
½ cup brandy
1 teaspoon salt
½ teaspoon pepper
½ teaspoon dried whole tarragon
½ teaspoon dried whole thyme
½ teaspoon dry mustard
2 bay leaves
1 (4- to 6-pound) beef tenderloin,
  trimmed
1 tablespoon vegetable oil
2 (8-ounce) packages Swiss cheese
  slices
Curly endive lettuce
Tomato roses (optional)
Party-size rolls or rye bread
Mayonnaise (optional)
Prepared horseradish (optional)
Coarse grained mustard (optional)

Combine wine, brandy, salt, pepper, tarragon, thyme, mustard, and bay leaves, stirring well. Place beef tenderloin in a large zip-top heavy-duty plastic bag; pour marinade over top and seal bag tightly. Place bag in a shallow roasting pan and refrigerate, marinating tenderloin at least 8 hours, turning occasionally.

Drain off and discard marinade. Place tenderloin on a greased rack in roasting pan; rub with oil and insert meat thermometer. Bake, uncovered, at 425° for 35 to 45 minutes or until thermometer registers 140° for rare. If desired, continue to bake at 425° until thermometer registers 150° for medium-rare or 160° for medium. After removing tenderloin from oven, let stand for 15 minutes.

Slice tenderloin, and cut each cheese slice into 4 triangles. Arrange sliced tenderloin, cheese triangles, and lettuce on serving platter. Garnish platter with tomato roses, if desired. Serve tenderloin slices, cheese triangles, and lettuce on party-size rolls; top with mayonnaise, horseradish, or coarse-grained mustard, if desired. Yield: 25 to 30 appetizer servings.

*o you know whether they've
sold the prize Turkey that was
hanging up there? Not the little prize Turkey: the big one?"*

*"What, the one as big as me?" re-
turned the boy.*

*"What a delightful boy!" said
Scrooge. "It's a pleasure to talk to him.
Yes, my buck!"*

*Opposite: Honey-glazed turkey afloat in sweet potato
stuffing will bring a golden glow to your table.*

HONEY-GLAZED TURKEY WITH SWEET POTATO STUFFING

2½ quarts water, divided
**6 medium sweet potatoes, peeled and
  cut into ½-inch cubes**
1 medium lemon
4 medium oranges, divided
2 large onions, chopped
¼ cup butter or margarine, melted
½ cup chicken broth
¼ cup lemon juice
¾ teaspoon salt
½ teaspoon pepper
**2 tablespoons butter or margarine,
  melted**
2 tablespoons brandy
1 teaspoon dry mustard
½ teaspoon ground cloves
**6 slices bread, toasted and cut into
  cubes**
1 (12- to 14-pound) turkey
¾ teaspoon salt
½ teaspoon pepper
2 tablespoons honey
Fresh parsley sprigs (optional)
Lemon rose (optional)
Lime rose (optional)

Bring 2 quarts water to a boil in a large
Dutch oven; add sweet potatoes. Cover and
boil 3 minutes; drain and set aside.

Remove rind in quarters from lemon and
2 oranges; cut rind into thin strips. Bring 1
cup water to a boil in a small saucepan;
add rind strips. Cover and boil 1 minute;

drain and set aside. Remove and discard
rind from remaining 2 oranges. Remove
white membrane from all 4 oranges. Section, seed, and chop oranges; set aside (reserve lemon for use in other recipes).

Sauté onions in ¼ cup butter in a large
Dutch oven until tender. Stir in sweet potatoes, rind, oranges, broth, lemon juice, ¾
teaspoon salt, and ½ teaspoon pepper.
Cover and cook over medium heat 10 minutes or until sweet potatoes are tender; remove from heat and cool slightly.

Combine 2 tablespoons melted butter,
brandy, mustard, and cloves; stir until
blended. Stir into sweet potato mixture.
Gently stir in bread cubes.

Remove giblets and neck from turkey
(reserve for giblet gravy, if desired). Rinse
turkey thoroughly and pat dry. Combine ¾
teaspoon salt and ½ teaspoon pepper; rub
over surface of turkey.

Spoon half of sweet potato stuffing into
cavity of turkey; close cavity with skewers.
Place remaining stuffing mixture in a
lightly greased 8-inch square baking dish;
set aside. Tie ends of legs to tail with
string or tuck them under flap of skin
around tail. Lift wingtips up and over back
so they are tucked under turkey securely.

Place turkey, breast side up, on rack in
shallow roasting pan containing remaining
1 cup water. Cover turkey with foil. Insert
meat thermometer through foil in meaty
part of thigh or breast, making sure it does
not touch bone or foil. Bake at 350° for 2
hours and 30 minutes.

Remove turkey from oven. Remove foil
and cut cord or band of skin holding drum-
stick ends to tail. Brush honey over surface
of turkey. Bake turkey and reserved stuffing, uncovered, at 325° for 30 minutes or
until thermometer registers 185° and stuffing is thoroughly heated.

Remove turkey and stuffing from oven.
Transfer turkey to serving platter; let stand
15 minutes before carving. Garnish with
fresh parsley sprigs and lemon and lime
roses, if desired. Serve with stuffing. Yield:
20 to 24 servings.

99

nd now two smaller Cratchits, a boy and girl, came tearing in, screaming that outside the baker's they had smelt the goose, and known it for their own; and basking in luxurious thoughts of sage and onion, these young Cratchits danced about the table.

Right: Tasty wreaths, as delicate as any Victorian legacy, these Holiday Potato Swirls are as wonderful to eat as they are to behold.

GOOSE WITH SAGE AND ONION
1 (9- to 10-pound) dressed goose
4 cups soft breadcrumbs
1 cup peeled, chopped cooking apple
½ cup golden raisins
½ cup chopped onion
⅓ cup butter or margarine, melted
2 teaspoons salt
1 to 1½ teaspoons rubbed sage
½ teaspoon dried whole rosemary
½ teaspoon pepper
Red and green grapes (optional)
Red and green apple wedges (optional)
Fresh sage sprigs (optional)

Remove giblets and neck from goose (reserve for giblet gravy, if desired). Rinse goose thoroughly and pat dry. Remove and discard excess fat; prick skin with a fork at 2-inch intervals.

Combine breadcrumbs and next 8 ingredients, stirring well. Spoon into cavity of goose; close with skewers. Fold neck skin over back and truss goose. Place goose, breast side up, on rack in a deep roasting pan. Insert meat thermometer in meaty part of thigh or breast, making sure it does not touch bone. Bake, uncovered, at 350° for 3 hours or until thermometer registers 185° and drumsticks move easily. If goose gets too brown, cover with foil. Discard excess fat as needed during baking.

Transfer goose to serving platter; let stand 15 minutes before carving. Garnish with grapes, apples, and sage, if desired. Yield: 6 to 8 servings.

HOLIDAY POTATO SWIRLS
4 medium baking potatoes
2 egg yolks, beaten
1 clove garlic, pressed
½ teaspoon salt
¼ teaspoon white pepper
¼ teaspoon freshly grated nutmeg
1 (8-ounce) carton commercial sour cream
2 tablespoons finely chopped fresh chives
Additional chopped fresh chives (optional)
Fresh chive bows (optional)

Wash potatoes; prick. Bake at 400° for 1 hour or until potatoes are done; let cool to touch. Cut potatoes in half lengthwise; scoop out pulp (reserve skins for use in other recipes). Place pulp in a large bowl;

mash with a fork until smooth. Add egg yolks, garlic, salt, pepper, and nutmeg; beat at low speed of an electric mixer until blended (mixture will be stiff). Spoon mixture into a decorating bag fitted with a large star tip; set aside.

Line 2 baking sheets with parchment paper; draw eight 2-inch circles on each. Beginning in center of each circle and working toward outer edges, pipe potato mixture in a continuous coil to form a base. Continue piping potato mixture, adding an additional coil around outer edges to form a raised border.

Bake at 400° for 20 minutes or until edges are lightly browned. Carefully remove from parchment paper and transfer to serving platter. Combine sour cream and 2 tablespoons chopped chives, stirring well. Spoon about 2 teaspoons sour cream mixture into center of each potato swirl. Garnish with additional chopped chives and a chive bow, if desired. Serve immediately. Yield: 8 servings.

SWEET CHESTNUT SOUFFLÉ
½ pound fresh chestnuts
3 cups water
Vegetable oil
½ cup butter or margarine
¼ cup plus 2 tablespoons all-purpose
  flour
¼ cup sugar
1½ cups milk
4 eggs, separated
1 tablespoon light rum
1 teaspoon vanilla extract
⅛ teaspoon cream of tartar
Powdered sugar
Dried apricot rose (optional)

Slash flat side of each chestnut with a shallow X. Combine chestnuts and water in a medium saucepan. Bring to a boil; cover, reduce heat, and simmer 25 minutes. Drain. Remove and discard chestnut shells and skins.

The poulterers' shops were still half open, and the fruiterers' were radiant in their glory. There were great round, pot-bellied baskets of chestnuts, shaped like the waistcoats of jolly old gentlemen, lolling at the doors, and tumbling out into the street in their apoplectic opulence.

Position knife blade in food processor bowl; add chestnut kernels. Cover and pulse 4 or 5 times until pureed, scraping sides of bowl, if necessary; set aside.

Cut a piece of aluminum foil long enough to fit around a 1-quart soufflé dish, allowing a 1-inch overlap; fold foil lengthwise into thirds. Lightly oil one side of foil and bottom of dish; wrap foil around dish, oiled side against dish, allowing it to extend 3 inches above rim to form a collar. Secure foil with string.

Melt butter in a medium saucepan over low heat. Combine flour and sugar; add to butter, stirring until smooth. Cook 1 minute, stirring constantly. Gradually add milk; cook over medium heat, stirring constantly, until mixture is thickened and bubbly.

Beat egg yolks until thick and lemon colored. Gradually stir about one-fourth of hot milk mixture into yolks; add to remaining hot milk mixture, stirring constantly. Transfer to a large bowl; stir in chestnuts, rum, and vanilla. Cool slightly.

Beat egg whites (at room temperature) and cream of tartar at high speed of an electric mixer until stiff peaks form; gently fold into chestnut mixture. Spoon into prepared dish. Bake at 350° for 1 hour or until puffed and golden. Remove collar from dish; sift powdered sugar over top. Garnish with an apricot rose, if desired. Serve immediately. Yield: 6 servings.

Tip: If a recipe calls for egg whites at room temperature, separate the whites from the yolks an hour ahead of preparation time.

Left: The youthful Scrooge was fortunate, indeed, if the cake his schoolmaster served was similar to this White Chocolate-Topped Fruit and Nut Loaf, packed full of cherries, dates, pistachios, and walnuts.

WHITE CHOCOLATE-TOPPED FRUIT AND NUT LOAF

¾ cup all-purpose flour
¾ cup sugar
½ teaspoon baking powder
½ teaspoon salt
2 cups chopped pitted dates
2 (10-ounce) jars maraschino cherries, drained and chopped
1 cup golden raisins
1 cup chopped pistachios
¾ cup chopped walnuts
½ cup raisins
4 eggs, beaten
1 tablespoon brandy
3 tablespoons brandy (optional)
6 ounces white chocolate, coarsely chopped
1½ teaspoons shortening
Additional chopped pistachios (optional)

Combine flour, sugar, baking powder, and salt in a large bowl, stirring well. Combine dates, cherries, golden raisins, 1 cup chopped pistachios, walnuts, and ½ cup raisins. Dredge in flour mixture. Stir in eggs and 1 tablespoon brandy.

Spoon batter into a greased and wax paper-lined 8½- x 4½- x 3-inch loafpan. Bake at 300° for 1 hour and 30 minutes or until a wooden pick inserted in center comes out clean; cool in pan 10 minutes. Remove from pan; remove and discard wax paper. Cool fruit and nut loaf completely on a wire rack.

103

Moisten several layers of cheesecloth with 3 tablespoons brandy, if desired; wrap loaf in cheesecloth. Store in an airtight container at least 1 week, remoistening cheesecloth as needed. Remove and discard cheesecloth; transfer loaf to serving platter.

Combine white chocolate and shortening in top of a double boiler; bring water to a boil. Reduce heat to low; cook, stirring constantly with a wire whisk, until melted. Remove from heat and drizzle over top of loaf. Sprinkle with additional chopped pistachios, if desired. Yield: 1 loaf.

MARVELOUS MINCEMEAT PIE
Double-Crust Pastry (recipe follows)
½ cup sugar
½ cup light corn syrup
¼ cup shortening
¼ teaspoon salt
1 (9-ounce) package condensed mincemeat, crumbled
2 eggs, beaten
¾ cup chopped pecans
½ cup raisins
3 tablespoons orange juice
1 teaspoon vanilla extract
3 pecan halves, toasted (optional)

Roll two-thirds of pastry to ⅛-inch thickness on a lightly floured surface; fit into a 9-inch pieplate. Trim edges, seal, and flute; set aside. Refrigerate remaining pastry.

Combine sugar, corn syrup, shortening, and salt in a small heavy saucepan; stir well and bring to a boil. Remove from heat. Combine mincemeat and next 5 ingredients in a medium bowl, stirring well; gradually stir in warm syrup mixture. Spoon into pastry shell.

Roll remaining one-third of pastry to ¼-inch thickness on a lightly floured surface; cut into ½-inch-wide strips. Beginning in center of pie and working toward outer sides, twist one strip and wind in a coil in center of pie. When this strip is gone, moisten end of strip and attach a second strip, pinching ends together. Twist strip and keep coiling over pie.

Continue joining, twisting, and coiling strips until surface of pie is covered. Moisten end of last strip and press into side of pastry shell. Bake at 350° for 45 minutes or until golden brown. Garnish center of pie with toasted pecan halves, if desired. Yield: one 9-inch pie.

Double-Crust Pastry:
2 cups all-purpose flour
1 teaspoon salt
⅔ cup plus 2 tablespoons shortening
4 to 5 tablespoons cold water

Combine flour and salt in a medium bowl; cut in shortening with a pastry blender until mixture resembles coarse meal. Sprinkle cold water, 1 tablespoon at a time, evenly over surface; and stir with a fork until the dry ingredients are moistened. Shape pastry into a ball; cover and refrigerate 30 minutes. Yield: pastry for one double-crust pie.

Opposite: Marvelous Mincemeat Pie, with its marvelous English tradition, is given a new twist on top with pastry that spirals out from the center to a deeply fluted outer crust. In the time of Henry VIII, the spices in mince pies represented the gifts of the Magi, and the pies were baked in rectangles to represent the Christ child's manger.

There were pears and apples, clustered high in blooming pyramids; there were bunches of grapes, made in the shopkeepers' benevolence to dangle from conspicuous hooks, that people's mouths might water gratis as they passed; there were piles of filberts, mossy and brown, recalling, in their fragrance, ancient walks among the woods, and pleasant shufflings ankle deep through withered leaves.

APPLES AND PEARS POACHED IN WINE

4 medium firm, ripe pears
4 medium cooking apples
⅓ cup lemon juice
2 cups rosé wine
2 cups water
1 cup sugar
Grated rind of 1 lemon
1 teaspoon lemon juice
1 (3½-inch) stick cinnamon
4 whole cloves
Ground cinnamon
Lemon rind strips (optional)

Peel pears and apples, removing core from bottom and leaving stem intact. Cut a thin slice from bottom of each, so fruit will stand upright; brush with ⅓ cup lemon juice to prevent browning. Set aside.

Combine wine and next 6 ingredients in a large Dutch oven. Bring to a boil; cook, stirring constantly, until sugar dissolves.

Add pears and apples, arranging upright. Cover, reduce heat, and simmer 15 minutes or just until fruit is tender but still holds its shape. Remove from heat; let fruit cool in wine mixture. Cover and refrigerate until chilled, spooning wine mixture over fruit occasionally.

Carefully transfer fruit to stemmed glasses, using a slotted spoon. Strain wine mixture to remove whole spices, reserving 1 cup; drizzle over fruit and sprinkle with cinnamon. Garnish with lemon rind strips, if desired. Yield: 8 servings.

Mrs. *Cratchit left the room alone—too nervous to bear witnesses—to take the pudding up, and bring it in.*

Suppose it should not be done enough! Suppose it should break in turning out! Suppose somebody should have got over the wall of the back-yard, and stolen it, while they were merry with the goose: a supposition at which the two young Cratchits became livid!

FLAMING BRANDY PLUM PUDDING

½ cup butter or margarine, softened
1½ cups firmly packed brown sugar
2 eggs, beaten
1 teaspoon rum extract
1 cup fine, dry breadcrumbs
1 cup all-purpose flour
1 teaspoon baking soda
½ teaspoon salt
1 teaspoon ground ginger
1 teaspoon ground allspice
1 teaspoon ground cinnamon
1 cup scraped, grated carrots
1 cup golden raisins
1 cup chopped pecans
½ cup chopped dried figs
½ cup chopped dried apricots
½ cup currants
½ cup plus 2 tablespoons brandy, divided
Cream Cheese-Brandy Sauce (recipe follows)

Cream butter in a large bowl; gradually add sugar, beating well. Add eggs and rum extract; beat well and set aside.

Combine breadcrumbs and next 6 ingredients in a large bowl, stirring well. Combine carrots and next 5 ingredients; dredge in breadcrumb mixture. Add to creamed mixture with ¼ cup brandy, stirring until combined.

Spoon mixture into a well-greased 1½-quart steamed pudding mold. Cover mold tightly and place on a shallow rack in a large, deep kettle with enough water to come halfway up sides of mold. Cover kettle and bring water to a boil; steam pudding 3 hours in continuously boiling water (add water as needed).

Let pudding stand 10 minutes; unmold onto serving plate. Pour 2 tablespoons brandy over hot pudding. Heat remaining ¼ cup brandy in a small, long-handled saucepan just until it produces fumes (do not let it come to a boil). Remove from heat and ignite brandy with a long match; carefully pour over pudding. Let flames die down. Cover plum pudding and refrigerate at least 8 hours. To serve, drizzle Cream Cheese-Brandy Sauce over top. Yield: 10 to 12 servings.

Cream Cheese-Brandy Sauce:
½ (3-ounce) package cream cheese, softened
1 tablespoon plus 1½ teaspoons brandy
1 cup sifted powdered sugar
1 teaspoon vanilla extract

Combine softened cream cheese and brandy in a small bowl; beat at medium speed of an electric mixer until fluffy. Gradually add powdered sugar and beat until blended. Stir in vanilla extract. Yield: about ½ cup.

Hallo! A great deal of steam! The pudding was out of the copper. . . . A smell like an eating-house, and a pastry cook's next door to each other, with a laundress's next door to that! That was the pudding. In half a minute Mrs. Cratchit entered: flushed, but smiling proudly: with the pudding, like a speckled cannon-ball, so hard and firm, blazing in half of half-a-quartern of ignited brandy, and bedight with Christmas holly stuck into the top.

Below: In Flaming Brandy Plum Pudding, all the elements are present—brown sugar, ginger, cinnamon, carrots, raisins, figs, brandy—including the most important ingredient of all . . . excitement!

The Movable Feast of Advent

Cranberry Welcome
Salmon Spread
Gingered Hearts of Palm Salad
Currant and Wine-Glazed Ham
Marinated Broccoli and Parsnips
Lemony Green Beans
Carrots Spectacular
Fancy Pinwheel Rolls
Advent Cake
Chocolate-Eggnog Swirl Pie

On the Sunday nearest to November 30, families at all points of the globe begin celebrating the Christmas season by observing Advent, the traditional period of preparation for the coming of the Christ child. This hum of activity extends to the kitchen, where busy cooks plan treats for guests, gifts of food, and the special Advent dinner, known as a "movable feast" since its date changes each year.

To help in your holiday plans, we offer this delicious menu. Whether you choose to celebrate your movable feast at the beginning of Advent or at any point up to the last Sunday before Christmas, you'll find all the elements for a particularly delectable meal here.

CRANBERRY WELCOME
1½ cups cranberry juice cocktail, chilled
3 cups cranapple juice, chilled
2 (6-ounce) cans pineapple juice, chilled
2 tablespoons lemon juice
1 quart rainbow sherbet, divided

Combine first 4 ingredients, stirring well. Pour into glasses; top each serving with a scoop of sherbet. Yield: 8 servings.

SALMON SPREAD
1 teaspoon unflavored gelatin
¼ cup cold water
1 (8-ounce) package cream cheese, softened
⅓ cup commercial sour cream
2 tablespoons dry sherry
½ teaspoon dried whole basil
1 (7¾-ounce) can salmon, drained, skinned, and flaked
1 (4¼-ounce) can tiny shrimp, rinsed, drained, and chopped
½ cup finely chopped celery
Celery leaves (optional)
Pita Bread Triangles (recipe follows)

Sprinkle unflavored gelatin over cold water in a small saucepan; let stand 5 minutes. Cook over low heat, stirring constantly, until dissolved.

Combine gelatin and next 4 ingredients in a medium bowl. Beat at medium speed of an electric mixer until smooth. Stir in salmon, shrimp, and chopped celery.

Spoon mixture into serving bowl; cover and refrigerate until thoroughly chilled. Garnish with celery leaves, if desired. Serve with Pita Bread Triangles. Yield: 3 cups.

Pita Bread Triangles:
4 (6-inch) whole wheat pita bread rounds
2 tablespoons butter or margarine, melted

Split each pita into 2 rounds; cut each round into 4 wedges. Place on baking sheets, smooth side down. Brush with butter and bake at 400° for 6 minutes or until crisp and lightly browned. Store in an airtight container. Yield: 32 triangles.

Opposite: In the holiday bustle, an Advent dinner offers a welcome moment to pause with family. Make it all the more special with the foods shown here: Currant and Wine-Glazed Ham, Carrots Spectacular, Marinated Broccoli and Parsnips, Lemony Green Beans, Fancy Pinwheel Rolls, Gingered Hearts of Palm Salad, and on the buffet, Advent Cake.

GINGERED HEARTS OF PALM SALAD

⅔ cup softened vanilla ice cream
¼ cup mayonnaise
¼ cup crunchy peanut butter
1 tablespoon pineapple juice
3 heads Bibb lettuce
2 (14-ounce) cans hearts of palm, drained and diagonally sliced into ½-inch slices
1 cup pineapple chunks, drained
1 cup thinly sliced celery
⅓ cup coarsely chopped pitted dates
2 tablespoons finely chopped crystallized ginger

Combine vanilla ice cream, mayonnaise, peanut butter, and pineapple juice, stirring until blended. Cover and refrigerate until thoroughly chilled.

Wash lettuce, trim core, and separate into leaves; discard wilted or discolored portions. Shake leaves to remove moisture; pat dry with paper towels.

Place lettuce leaves on individual salad plates. Arrange hearts of palm and pineapple chunks over lettuce. Sprinkle with celery and dates; top with ice cream mixture and sprinkle with crystallized ginger. Yield: 8 servings.

CURRANT AND WINE-GLAZED HAM

1 (6- to 7-pound) smoked fully cooked
  ham half
½ cup Chablis or other dry white wine
2 tablespoons orange juice
2 teaspoons cornstarch
⅓ cup red currant jelly, divided
1 tablespoon butter or margarine
Fresh parsley sprigs (optional)
Baby corn on the cob (optional)
Spiced peaches (optional)
Spiced crabapples (optional)

Remove hard outer crust of ham; score
fat on ham in a diamond pattern. Place
ham, fat side up, on a rack in a shallow
roasting pan; insert meat thermometer,
making sure it does not touch fat or bone.
Bake, uncovered, at 325° for 1½ hours; remove ham from oven and set aside.

Combine wine, juice, and cornstarch in a
small saucepan; stir until dissolved. Add
half of currant jelly; cook over low heat,
stirring constantly, until thick and bubbly.
Add remaining jelly and butter; cook over
low heat, stirring frequently, until melted.

Brush half of currant and wine glaze
over ham; set remaining glaze aside. Bake
ham at 325° an additional 30 minutes or
until thermometer registers 140°. Baste
every 10 minutes with remaining glaze.
Transfer to serving platter and garnish
with parsley, corn, peaches, and crabapples, if desired. Yield: 12 to 14 servings.

MARINATED BROCCOLI
AND PARSNIPS

1½ pounds fresh broccoli
4 cups scraped, cubed parsnips
1 cup cherry tomato halves
⅓ cup vegetable oil
⅓ cup red wine vinegar
¼ cup sliced green onions
1 tablespoon sugar
⅛ teaspoon salt
4 dashes hot sauce

Trim off large leaves of broccoli. Remove
tough ends of lower stalks and wash broccoli thoroughly; cut broccoli into 2-inch
spears. Arrange broccoli in a steaming rack
with stalks to center of rack. Place over
boiling water; cover and steam 5 minutes
or until crisp-tender. Drain and set aside.

Place parsnips in a large saucepan and
cover with water. Bring to a boil; cover, reduce heat, and simmer 8 minutes or until
crisp-tender. Drain.

Combine broccoli, parsnips, and tomato
halves in a large bowl. Combine oil, vinegar, onions, sugar, salt, and hot sauce, stirring well; pour over vegetables and toss
gently to coat. Cover and refrigerate 1
hour. Serve with slotted spoon. Yield: 8
servings.

LEMONY GREEN BEANS

2 pounds fresh green beans
1½ quarts water
1 teaspoon salt
¼ cup plus 2 tablespoons butter or
  margarine, divided
2 tablespoons sesame seeds
Grated rind and juice of 2 lemons
1 (4-ounce) jar sliced pimiento,
  drained
⅓ cup sliced almonds, toasted

Wash green beans, trim ends, and remove strings. Cut green beans into 3-inch
pieces. Combine green beans, water, and
salt in a small Dutch oven. Bring to a boil;
cover, reduce heat, and simmer 20 minutes
or until tender. Drain off liquid. Set aside
and keep warm.

Melt 1 tablespoon butter in a small
saucepan; add sesame seeds and cook over
medium-low heat, stirring constantly, until
browned. Add remaining ¼ cup plus 1 tablespoon butter and continue to cook over
medium-low heat until butter melts. Stir in
rind and juice. Pour butter mixture over reserved green beans in Dutch oven, tossing
gently to coat. Transfer to serving bowl; arrange pimiento and almonds over top.
Serve hot. Yield: 8 servings.

CARROTS SPECTACULAR

½ cup water
½ teaspoon salt
3 large carrots, scraped and thinly
  sliced
1 tablespoon butter or margarine,
  melted
3 cups shredded carrots
1 medium baking potato, peeled and
  cubed
2 eggs
¼ cup commercial sour cream
1 teaspoon grated lemon rind
¼ to ½ teaspoon dried whole basil
2 to 3 dashes hot sauce
¾ teaspoon salt
⅛ teaspoon white pepper
Fresh basil sprig (optional)

Combine water and ½ teaspoon salt in a
medium saucepan; bring to a boil and add
sliced carrots. Cover, reduce heat, and simmer 3 minutes or until crisp-tender; drain
and set aside.

Brush a 9-inch round cakepan with
melted butter. Beginning in center of pan

*Above: Divine Chocolate-Eggnog Swirl Pie and Ad-
vent Cake provide a grand finale for a meaningful
meal. (The cake offers an extra treat: baked inside
are a pea and bean. Whoever gets a slice with one of
them in it will have good luck in the coming year.)*

*Behind the desserts is an evergreen Advent
wreath. Its circle represents eternity, and each Sunday, another of the four candles is lit. First comes
the Prophesy Candle, second is the Bethlehem Candle, third is the Shepherd's, and fourth is the Angel's
Candle. Lighting the center candle, which represents
Christ, completes the ceremony on Christmas day.*

and working toward outer edges, arrange
carrot slices in petal fashion, slightly overlapping edges, to cover bottom of pan.
Press slices around sides of pan. Cover and
refrigerate 30 minutes.

Combine shredded carrots and potato in
a large saucepan; add water to cover. Bring
to a boil; cover, reduce heat, and simmer
15 minutes or until tender. Drain and set
aside.

Combine eggs, sour cream, rind, dried
whole basil, hot sauce, ¾ teaspoon salt,
and white pepper in container of electric

111

blender or food processor. Add half of carrot-potato mixture; cover and process until smooth. Add remaining carrot-potato mixture, processing until smooth. Cover and refrigerate until thoroughly chilled.

Carefully spoon refrigerated mixture into carrot-lined pan, smoothing top with a spatula. Bake at 350° for 45 minutes or until a wooden pick inserted in center comes out clean; cool in pan 15 minutes. Using a sharp knife, gently loosen carrot slices from edges of pan. Carefully invert onto serving platter. Garnish with a fresh basil sprig, if desired. Cut into wedges and serve warm. Yield: 8 servings.

FANCY PINWHEEL ROLLS
2¼ cups all-purpose flour, divided
1 package dry yeast
1 cup milk
2 tablespoons vegetable oil
2 tablespoons honey
1 teaspoon salt
1 egg, beaten
1 cup whole wheat flour
2 (8-ounce) packages cream cheese, softened
1 teaspoon onion powder
2 teaspoons water
1 egg yolk
1 tablespoon milk

Combine 1½ cups all-purpose flour and yeast in a large bowl, stirring well; set aside.

Combine milk and next 3 ingredients in a small saucepan; cook over low heat until very warm (120° to 130°). Remove from heat and add to reserved flour mixture. Add egg and beat at low speed of an electric mixer for 30 seconds, scraping sides of bowl. Increase speed to high and continue to beat 3 minutes. Stir in remaining ¾ cup all-purpose flour and whole wheat flour to make a moderately stiff dough.

Turn dough out onto a floured surface; knead until smooth and elastic (about 8 to 10 minutes). Place dough in a greased

bowl, turning to grease top. Cover and let rise in a warm place (85°), free from drafts, 1 hour or until doubled in bulk.

Punch dough down and turn out onto a lightly floured surface; cover and let rest 10 minutes. Divide dough in half. Roll each half into an 18- x 10-inch rectangle. Combine cream cheese, onion powder, and water, beating at low speed of an electric mixer until smooth; gently spread over rectangles. Roll up each rectangle, jellyroll fashion, beginning at long side; pinch edges together to seal. Cut each roll into ½-inch slices. Place 2 slices of dough, side by side with a cut side down, on a greased baking sheet. Center a third slice of dough, cut side down, on top to form 1 pinwheel roll. Repeat procedure with remaining slices. Cover and let rise in a warm place (85°), free from drafts, 30 minutes or until doubled in bulk. Combine egg yolk and milk, stirring well; gently brush over rolls. Bake at 375° for 12 minutes or until golden brown. Yield: 2 dozen.

ADVENT CAKE
1 cup raisins
1 cup currants
1 cup ground almonds
1 cup coarsely chopped candied pineapple
½ cup coarsely chopped candied red cherries
¾ cup bourbon
1½ cups butter or margarine, softened
1½ cups sugar
6 eggs
3 cups all-purpose flour
1 teaspoon ground ginger
1 teaspoon ground cinnamon
½ teaspoon ground nutmeg
1 dried pinto bean (optional)
1 dried black-eyed pea (optional)
1 (8-ounce) package cream cheese, softened
1 tablespoon milk
Sliced almonds, toasted

Combine first 6 ingredients, stirring well; cover and let stand at least 8 hours.

Cream butter in a large bowl; gradually add sugar, beating at medium speed of an electric mixer until light and fluffy. Add eggs, one at a time, beating well after each addition. Sift together flour and spices; gradually add to creamed mixture, mixing well. Stir in reserved fruit mixture.

Spoon batter into a greased and wax paper-lined 9-inch springform pan. At random, press bean and pea just below surface of batter, if desired. Bake at 300° for 2 hours or until a wooden pick inserted in center comes out clean; cool completely in pan. Remove sides of springform pan; remove and discard wax paper from cake.

Combine cream cheese and milk; beat at low speed of an electric mixer until blended. Spoon into a decorating bag fitted with a medium star tip; pipe rosettes over top of cake. Insert almonds into cream cheese rosettes. Yield: one 9-inch cake.

CHOCOLATE-EGGNOG SWIRL PIE
¾ cup sugar
⅓ cup all-purpose flour
2 cups milk
1 cup commercial canned eggnog
1 egg, beaten
1 teaspoon vanilla extract
2 (1-ounce) squares unsweetened
  chocolate
Star Cookie Crust (recipe follows)
¼ cup whipping cream

Combine sugar and flour in a large saucepan. Stir in milk and eggnog; cook over medium heat, stirring constantly, until thickened and bubbly. Gradually stir about ½ cup of hot mixture into egg; add to remaining hot mixture, stirring constantly with a wire whisk. Continue to cook over medium heat, stirring constantly, 2 minutes; remove from heat.

Add vanilla to 2 cups of custard mixture, stirring well; set aside. Place chocolate in top of a double boiler; bring water to a boil. Reduce heat to low; cook until chocolate melts. Add chocolate to remaining custard mixture in saucepan; stir well. Pour chocolate custard mixture into Star Cookie Crust. Pour vanilla custard mixture over top, gently spreading to edges of crust; cut through custard mixtures with a knife to create a marbled effect. Cover and refrigerate at least 8 hours.

Beat whipping cream until stiff peaks form. Spoon into center of pie; arrange stars from Star Cookie Crust in whipping cream. Yield: one 9-inch pie.

Star Cookie Crust:
2 cups all-purpose flour
3 tablespoons sugar
Dash of salt
3 tablespoons shortening
2 eggs, beaten
1 (1-ounce) square unsweetened
  chocolate

Combine flour, sugar, and salt in a medium bowl, stirring well. Cut in shortening with a pastry blender until mixture resembles coarse meal. Add beaten eggs, and stir with a fork until all ingredients are thoroughly moistened.

Roll two-thirds of pastry to ⅛-inch thickness on a lightly floured surface. Place in a 9-inch pieplate; trim excess pastry and crimp edges. Lightly prick bottom and sides of pastry shell. Bake at 450° (with pie weights) for 5 minutes; remove weights and bake an additional 4 minutes or until golden brown.

Roll remaining pastry to ⅛-inch thickness on lightly floured surface. Cut out with a 2-inch star-shaped cookie cutter and place on an ungreased cookie sheet. Bake at 400° for 6 minutes or until lightly browned. Remove to a wire rack to cool.

Place chocolate in top of a double boiler; bring water to a boil. Reduce heat to low; cook until chocolate melts. Drizzle chocolate over stars; allow chocolate to harden. Yield: one 9-inch pastry shell and 16 stars.

Celebrate with Champagne and Cheesecake

From early December through New Year's Eve, any night is a good night for a champagne and cheesecake party. The elegant and festive fare sets the mood for a memorable intimate gathering. Bring out the crystal and silver, fill your table with Cheesecake Brownies, Amaretto Macaroon Cheesecake, and Champagne Punch, and let the magic unfold.

Above: The sweets connoisseur will swoon at this array. Clockwise from back are Champagne Punch, Cream Cheese and Pecan Cookies, Amaretto Macaroon Cheesecake, Miniature Cheesecakes, Fruit Basket Cheesecake, Cheesecake Brownies, and White Chocolate Cheesecake.

CHAMPAGNE PUNCH
1 cup orange juice
1 cup lemon juice
1½ cups sugar
2 (25.4-ounce) bottles dry white wine, chilled
2 (25.4-ounce) bottles champagne, chilled
Fruity Ice Ring (optional) (recipe follows)

Combine juice and sugar in a medium-size heavy saucepan. Bring to a boil; reduce heat and simmer, stirring constantly, until sugar dissolves. Remove from heat; cover and refrigerate until thoroughly chilled.

To serve, pour juice mixture into a large punch bowl. Stir in wine and champagne. Add Fruity Ice Ring to punch bowl, if desired. Yield: about 3½ quarts.

Fruity Ice Ring:
2 cups crushed ice
1 medium-size Red Delicious apple, cored and sliced lengthwise into 12 wedges
Lemon juice
2 medium lemons, sliced lengthwise into 8 wedges
1 medium lime, sliced lengthwise into 8 wedges
1 medium orange, sliced lengthwise into 8 wedges
1½ cups orange juice

Arrange crushed ice evenly in bottom of a 6½-cup ring mold. Brush apple wedges with lemon juice; remove and discard seeds from remaining lemon, lime, and orange wedges. Arrange fruit attractively over ice, positioning wedges to stand on end. Carefully pour orange juice around fruit; freeze at least 8 hours.

Place mold in a large bowl of warm water for 5 seconds to loosen ring; carefully unmold. Immediately place ice ring, fruit side up, in a filled punch bowl. Yield: one 9-inch ice ring.

FRUIT BASKET CHEESECAKE

1⅔ cups gingersnap cookie crumbs
½ cup finely chopped walnuts
¼ cup plus 2 tablespoons butter or
 margarine, melted
2 (3-ounce) packages lemon-flavored
 gelatin
2 cups boiling water
1 pint vanilla ice cream, softened
2 (8-ounce) packages cream cheese,
 softened
1 cup whipping cream
⅔ cup strawberry preserves
1 (3-ounce) package cream cheese,
 softened
¼ cup butter or margarine, softened
1 teaspoon vanilla extract
2 cups sifted powdered sugar
About 1 cup fresh strawberries, hulled
 and quartered (optional)

Combine gingersnap crumbs and walnuts in a small bowl, stirring well. Add
melted butter; stir until combined. Press
mixture into bottom and 2 inches up sides

*Above: Strawberries and cream, one of the more per-
fect pairings in the world of food, transport this
beautiful Fruit Basket Cheesecake into the realm of
delicious bliss.*

of a 9-inch springform pan. Bake at 375°
for 5 minutes; cool completely.

Dissolve gelatin in boiling water in a medium bowl. Add softened ice cream; stir
until melted. Refrigerate until mixture is
the consistency of unbeaten egg white.

Place 8-ounce packages cream cheese in
a large bowl; beat at low speed of an electric mixer until fluffy. Gradually add whipping cream; beat until blended. Add gelatin
mixture, beating well. Pour into prepared
pan; cover and chill at least 8 hours.

Gently spread preserves over top of
cheesecake, leaving a ½-inch margin
around outer edges. Cover and refrigerate
at least 1 hour to set preserves. Combine
3-ounce package cream cheese, softened
butter, and vanilla in a small bowl; cream
well. Gradually add sugar; beat well at low

115

speed of electric mixer. Cover and refrigerate 1 hour or until chilled. Spoon frosting mixture into a decorating bag fitted with a small comb-shaped tip; set aside.

Loosen sides of cheesecake from springform pan with a spatula. Carefully remove outer rim of pan and place cheesecake on serving plate. Pipe 6 evenly spaced rows of frosting over surface of cheesecake; give cheesecake a quarter-turn and repeat piping procedure to achieve a basket-weave effect. Changing to a medium star tip, pipe a shell design around outer edges of cheesecake. Arrange strawberries around base of cheesecake, if desired. Refrigerate until serving time. Yield: one 9-inch cheesecake.

AMARETTO MACAROON CHEESECAKE

1 tablespoon butter or margarine, softened
¾ cup amaretto macaroon cookie crumbs, divided
4 (8-ounce) packages cream cheese, softened
1¼ cups sugar
4 eggs
½ teaspoon grated lemon rind
¼ cup plus 1 tablespoon amaretto
¼ cup plus 2 tablespoons finely chopped almonds, toasted and divided

Grease a 9- x 5- x 3-inch loafpan with butter; sprinkle ¼ cup macaroon crumbs over bottom and sides of pan and press into place. Chill while completing recipe.

Place cream cheese in a large bowl; beat at low speed of an electric mixer until fluffy. Gradually add sugar, beating until light and fluffy. Add eggs, one at a time, beating well after each addition. Add rind and amaretto; mix well.

Sprinkle 2 tablespoons macaroon crumbs over bottom and sides of pan. Pour cream cheese mixture into pan; cut through mixture with a knife to remove air bubbles. Place loafpan in a 13- x 9- x 2-inch baking

pan; add 1½ inches of hot water to pan. Bake at 325° for 1 hour and 15 minutes or until set. Remove pans from oven; let stand 20 minutes. Remove loafpan from water and transfer to a cooling rack. Cool at least 2 hours.

To remove cheesecake, slowly tilt loafpan toward one side to form an air pocket between cheesecake and pan. Center a serving platter over top of pan and carefully invert. Coat sides of cheesecake with 3 tablespoons macaroon crumbs.

Cut four 8- x 1½-inch strips of wax paper; place diagonally across top of cake at 1½-inch intervals. Sprinkle remaining 3 tablespoons macaroon crumbs over top. Carefully remove wax paper strips, discarding 1 strip and gently placing remaining 3 strips over areas just sprinkled. Sprinkle 3 tablespoons toasted almonds over top; carefully remove and discard strips. Sprinkle remaining 3 tablespoons toasted almonds around base of cheesecake. Cover and refrigerate at least 8 hours. Cut into slices to serve. Yield: 12 servings.

WHITE CHOCOLATE CHEESECAKE

1½ cups graham cracker crumbs
¼ cup finely chopped pecans
3 tablespoons brown sugar
2 tablespoons cocoa, sifted
⅓ cup butter or margarine, melted
6 ounces white chocolate, coarsely chopped
½ cup whipping cream
2 (8-ounce) packages cream cheese, softened
¾ cup sugar
4 eggs
¼ cup whipping cream
2 teaspoons vanilla extract, divided
1½ cups commercial sour cream
¼ cup sugar
Shaved unsweetened chocolate
White and dark chocolate leaves

Combine graham cracker crumbs, pecans, brown sugar, and cocoa in a small

bowl, stirring well. Add butter; stir until combined. Press mixture into bottom and 1¼ inches up sides of a 9-inch springform pan. Bake at 350° for 6 minutes; cool.

Combine chopped white chocolate and ½ cup whipping cream in top of a double boiler; bring water to a boil. Reduce heat to low; cook, stirring constantly with a wire whisk, until melted. Let cool.

Place cream cheese in a large bowl; beat at low speed of an electric mixer until fluffy. Gradually add ¾ cup sugar, beating well. Add eggs, one at a time, beating well after each addition. Add ¼ cup cream and 1 teaspoon vanilla to cooled chocolate, stirring until blended; stir into cream cheese mixture. Pour mixture into prepared pan and bake at 350° for 1 hour or until cheesecake is almost set. Remove from oven; cool for 15 minutes.

Above: As delicate as a snowy bit of the forest floor, White Chocolate Cheesecake is a chocoholic's fantasy come true. To make the cluster of chocolate leaves, brush melted chocolate on a real leaf, let it harden, and then gently remove the natural mold.

Combine sour cream, ¼ cup sugar, and remaining 1 teaspoon vanilla; beat at medium speed of an electric mixer until blended. Gently spread mixture over cheesecake. Return to oven; bake at 425° for 10 minutes or until set. Let cool; cover and refrigerate at least 8 hours.

Loosen sides of cheesecake from springform pan with a spatula. Carefully remove outer rim of pan and place cheesecake on serving plate. Sprinkle shaved chocolate over top and garnish with chocolate leaves. Yield: one 9-inch cheesecake.

CREAM CHEESE AND PECAN COOKIES

¼ cup plus 2 tablespoons butter or
  margarine, softened
1 (3-ounce) package cream cheese,
  softened
⅓ cup sugar
1¼ cups all-purpose flour
½ cup finely chopped pecans
About 3½ dozen pecan halves

Combine butter and cream cheese in a medium bowl; cream well. Gradually add sugar, beating until light and fluffy. Add flour and mix well. Stir in chopped pecans.

Shape dough into 1-inch balls; place 2 inches apart on ungreased cookie sheets. Dip a flat-bottomed glass in water; slightly flatten each ball of dough. Gently press a pecan half into center of each cookie. Bake at 325° for 10 minutes or until lightly browned. Cool 2 minutes and remove from cookie sheets; cool completely on wire racks. Yield: about 3½ dozen.

CHEESECAKE BROWNIES

1 (8-ounce) package cream cheese,
  softened
½ cup butter or margarine, softened
2 cups sugar
4 eggs
2 teaspoons instant coffee granules
2 teaspoons hot water
1 cup all-purpose flour
½ cup cocoa
½ teaspoon baking powder
½ teaspoon salt
1½ teaspoons vanilla extract
1 cup chopped walnuts
1 (3-ounce) package cream cheese,
  softened
1 tablespoon milk
Crystallized violets (optional)

Combine first 2 ingredients in a large bowl; cream well. Gradually add sugar, beating well at low speed of an electric mixer. Add eggs, one at a time, beating well after each addition. Dissolve coffee granules in hot water; add to mixture, beating until blended. Combine flour and next 3 ingredients; add to mixture, beating well. Stir in vanilla and walnuts.

Pour batter into a greased and floured 13- x 9- x 2-inch baking pan. Bake at 350° for 35 minutes or until a wooden pick inserted in center comes out clean. Cool completely and cut into squares.

Combine 3-ounce package cream cheese and milk; beat at low speed of mixer until blended and spoon mixture into a decorating bag fitted with a medium star tip. Pipe a rosette on each brownie. Garnish with violets, if desired. Yield: 2 dozen.

MINIATURE CHEESECAKES

½ cup gingersnap cookie crumbs
2 tablespoons butter or margarine,
  melted
1 (8-ounce) package cream cheese,
  softened
¼ cup sugar
1 egg
½ teaspoon vanilla extract
3 tablespoons pineapple preserves
3 tablespoons mint-flavored apple jelly
3 tablespoons cherry preserves
Candied red and green cherries

Combine crumbs and butter; stir well. Line 1¾-inch muffin pans with miniature paper liners. Spoon 1 teaspoon mixture into each liner; gently press into bottom.

Place cream cheese in a small bowl; beat at low speed of electric mixer until fluffy. Gradually add sugar, beating until fluffy. Add egg and vanilla, mixing well; spoon into liners. Bake at 350° for 10 minutes.

Place pineapple preserves in a small saucepan; cook over low heat just until melted. Spoon 1 teaspoon melted preserves on each of 8 cheesecakes. Repeat procedure with mint-flavored apple jelly, cherry preserves, and remaining cheesecakes. Garnish with cherries. Cover and refrigerate until chilled. Yield: 2 dozen.

Fast and Fabulous Meals

Even during your crunch days, taste buds needn't suffer. From appetizers to entrees and desserts, you'll find dishes here that will come together fast and be as delicious as they are convenient.

Above: Roasted Red Pepper Endive Boats provide smooth sailing in the quest for healthy food that's good to eat.

ROASTED RED PEPPER ENDIVE BOATS
1 (7-ounce) jar roasted red peppers, drained
½ (2-ounce) can anchovies, drained and rinsed
3 large green olives, pitted
1 tablespoon chopped fresh parsley
¼ teaspoon olive oil
¼ teaspoon lemon juice
Dash of salt
Dash of freshly ground pepper
4 small heads Belgian endive
1 (4½-ounce) package fresh alfalfa sprouts, washed and drained

Combine first 4 ingredients in container of an electric blender or food processor; cover and process until finely chopped, scraping sides of container, if necessary. Add oil, lemon juice, salt, and pepper; process until blended. Cover and refrigerate until thoroughly chilled.

Arrange endive leaves on serving platter. Place a small bunch of alfalfa sprouts on stem end of each leaf. Spoon red pepper mixture into a decorating bag fitted with a large round tip. Pipe about 1 heaping teaspoonful mixture at base of alfalfa sprouts. Serve immediately. Yield: about 2 dozen.

CHRISTMAS APPLES WITH CRANAPPLE ICE
4 medium Granny Smith apples
Lemon juice
⅓ cup sugar
⅔ cup water
1¾ cups cranapple juice, chilled

Cut a ½-inch slice from top of each apple, leaving stem intact; reserve apple tops. Hollow each apple to within 1 inch of bottom, leaving a ½-inch shell. Cut a ¼-inch slice from bottom of each apple so that it will stand upright. Sprinkle inside of apple tops and shells with lemon juice; freeze apples while completing recipe.

Combine sugar and water in a small heavy saucepan; cook over high heat, stirring constantly, until sugar dissolves. Remove sugar syrup from heat and cool.

Combine syrup and cranapple juice, stirring until blended; pour into a freezer tray. Cover and freeze until firm; stir several times during freezing process.

To serve, position knife blade in food processor bowl; add frozen mixture and top with cover. Process until smooth. Mound cranapple ice in frozen apple shells; place apple tops on side of mound. Serve immediately or store in freezer until serving time. Yield: 4 servings.

119

ROASTED RACK OF LAMB

1 (2¾-pound) rack of lamb (8 chops)
2 cups soft breadcrumbs
½ cup minced fresh parsley
¼ cup plus 2 tablespoons minced
  fresh basil
¼ cup plus 2 tablespoons
  coarse-grained mustard
2 cloves garlic, minced
½ teaspoon salt
½ teaspoon pepper
Fresh parsley sprigs (optional)
Fresh basil sprigs (optional)
1 (10-ounce) jar preserved kumquats,
  drained (optional)

Place lamb, fat side up, on a greased

Above: Pop this lamb in the oven and get on with your holiday activities. Roasted Rack of Lamb lets you pamper your family even when time is short.

rack in a shallow roasting pan. Place a folded strip of aluminum foil over exposed ends of ribs. Bake at 400° for 40 minutes.

Combine breadcrumbs and next 6 ingredients, stirring well. Pat mixture over top and sides of rack. Insert meat thermometer, making sure it does not touch fat or bone. Bake at 350° for 10 minutes or until thermometer registers 145° (medium-rare). Transfer to serving platter and garnish with parsley, basil, and kumquats, if desired. Let stand 5 minutes before slicing. Yield: 4 servings.

CHOCOLATE-MINT POTS DE CRÈME

**2 (4-ounce) packages sweet baking
  chocolate**
1 cup whipping cream
4 egg yolks, beaten
½ teaspoon mint extract
**2 (1-ounce) squares semisweet
  chocolate**
¼ cup whipping cream, whipped
Grated orange rind (optional)

Place sweet baking chocolate in top of a
double boiler; bring water to a boil. Reduce
heat to low; cook until chocolate melts.
Gradually add 1 cup whipping cream, stirring constantly with a wire whisk, until
smooth.

Gradually stir about one-fourth of chocolate-cream mixture into egg yolks; add to
remaining chocolate-cream mixture, stirring constantly with a wire whisk. Continue to cook over simmering water until
thickened. Stir in mint extract. Spoon into
small cordial glasses or demitasse cups.
Cover and refrigerate at least 1 hour.

Place semisweet chocolate in top of a
double boiler; bring water to a boil. Reduce
heat to low; cook until chocolate melts.
Spoon melted chocolate into a decorating
bag fitted with a small round tip. Pipe six
small random designs onto a wax paper-
lined baking sheet. Freeze 5 minutes or
until chocolate hardens. Spoon a small
amount of whipped cream in center of
each pot de crème; sprinkle with orange
rind, if desired. Carefully remove chocolate
designs from wax paper and insert into
whipped cream. Yield: 6 servings.

*Above: When unexpected friends stop by, dazzle them
with Chocolate-Mint Pots de Crème. This wonderful
concoction belies its easy preparation. And the garnish of whipped cream topped with grated orange
rind and a chocolate "squiggle" transforms this
sweet treat into a work of art. For added panache,
serve it in a mixed collection of porcelain demitasse
cups like those shown here.*

PORK CHOPS WITH PECANS AND CURRANTS

¼ cup currants
3 tablespoons orange juice
2 tablespoons dry sherry
½ cup cider vinegar
**¼ cup plus 3 tablespoons firmly
  packed brown sugar, divided**
¼ cup sugar
**4 (1-inch-thick) center-cut loin pork
  chops (about 1¾ pounds)**
1 tablespoon vegetable oil
⅓ cup small pecan halves
**2 tablespoons butter or margarine,
  melted**
1 teaspoon grated lemon rind
Dried-apricot rose (optional)

Combine first 3 ingredients; stir well and
set aside.

Combine vinegar, ¼ cup brown sugar,
and sugar, stirring until sugar dissolves.
Place pork chops in a shallow container;
pour vinegar mixture over top. Cover and
refrigerate 15 minutes, turning chops after
8 minutes. Remove chops and discard vinegar mixture.

Heat oil in a large skillet over medium

heat. Add pork chops; cover and cook 12 minutes or until chops are tender, turning after 6 minutes. Drain pork chops on paper towels. Transfer to serving platter and keep warm. Drain off pan drippings; wipe skillet with paper towels.

Sauté pecans in butter in skillet until toasted. Stir in remaining 3 tablespoons brown sugar and lemon rind; cook over medium-high heat until sugar dissolves. Gradually stir in currant mixture; continue to cook over medium-high heat until mixture is thickened and bubbly. Spoon mixture over pork chops; garnish with an apricot rose, if desired. Yield: 4 servings.

WHOLE WHEAT PANCAKE AND SAUSAGE PLATTER

1 (12-ounce) package brown-and-serve sausage links
¾ cup all-purpose flour
¾ cup whole wheat flour
¼ cup sugar
1 tablespoon baking powder
1 teaspoon salt
2 cups buttermilk
2 eggs, beaten
3 tablespoons vegetable oil
1 cup maple syrup
Butter or margarine

Cook sausage links according to package directions; drain on paper towels.

Combine all-purpose flour and next 4 ingredients in a medium bowl. Combine buttermilk, eggs, and oil, stirring until blended; add to dry ingredients, stirring just until moistened (batter will be lumpy).

For each pancake, pour about ⅓ cup batter onto a hot, lightly greased griddle or skillet. Turn pancakes when tops are covered with bubbles and edges are browned. Place syrup in a small container in center of a serving platter. Arrange pancakes, with edges overlapping, in a circular pattern around syrup; tuck a sausage link under edge of each pancake. Serve immediately with butter. Yield: 6 servings.

ENDIVE AND WALNUT SALAD

4 small heads Belgian endive
1 medium carrot, scraped and finely shredded
¼ cup coarsely chopped walnuts
¼ cup olive oil
2 tablespoons balsamic vinegar
⅛ teaspoon salt
Freshly ground pepper to taste

Slice endive leaves lengthwise into thin strips. Arrange strips on individual salad plates and sprinkle with carrot.

Sauté chopped walnuts in olive oil in a small skillet until lightly browned, and stir in balsamic vinegar. Remove from heat and pour dressing over salads. Sprinkle with salt and pepper to taste. Yield: 4 servings.

HOLIDAY RICE-MUSHROOM BAKE

1 cup sliced fresh mushrooms
½ cup chopped green pepper
½ cup chopped sweet red pepper
⅓ cup chopped onion
¼ cup butter or margarine, melted
2 cups regular rice, uncooked
2 (10¾-ounce) cans chicken broth, undiluted
1 cup water
¼ cup grated Parmesan cheese
1 tablespoon white wine Worcestershire sauce
½ teaspoon white pepper
Chopped fresh parsley

Sauté first 4 ingredients in butter in a large skillet until tender. Stir in rice, broth, water, Parmesan cheese, white wine Worcestershire sauce, and pepper. Pour into a lightly greased 8-inch square baking dish. Cover and bake at 350° for 1 hour or until all liquid is absorbed.

Cut three 12- x 1½-inch strips of wax paper; place diagonally across top of casserole at 1½-inch intervals. Sprinkle parsley over top. Carefully remove and discard wax paper. Yield: 8 servings.

Spectacular Candies And Delectable Gifts

Christmas doesn't quite seem like Christmas until the sweets and attractively packaged gifts of food emerge. If you're looking for new recipes, try these. Candy-Coated Pretzel Wreaths, Italian-Seasoned Dressing and Croutons, Marshmallow Snowmen, and Raspberry Truffles are just a few of the show-stopping offerings.

MARSHMALLOW SNOWMEN
4 cups sugar
1¾ cups water, divided
4 envelopes unflavored gelatin
1 teaspoon almond extract
½ cup powdered sugar
½ cup cornstarch
Flaked coconut
Wooden picks
Assorted candies
Red maraschino cherries, slivered

Combine 4 cups sugar and 1 cup water in a small Dutch oven, stirring well. Cover; let stand at room temperature 30 minutes.

Combine gelatin and remaining ¾ cup water in a large bowl, stirring well. Cover; let stand at room temperature 30 minutes.

Bring sugar mixture to a boil; reduce heat to medium and cook, stirring frequently, until sugar dissolves. Wash off sugar crystals from sides of pan, using a brush dipped in cold water. Continue to cook over medium heat, without stirring, until mixture reaches firm ball stage (244°). Remove from heat and pour hot sugar syrup in a thin stream over gelatin mixture, beating constantly at medium speed of a heavy-duty electric mixer. Continue to beat at medium speed 30 minutes; add almond extract, beating well.

Sift together powdered sugar and cornstarch into a 15- x 10- x 1-inch jellyroll pan. Spread marshmallow mixture evenly in pan; cover lightly with wax paper. Let

Above: Get the kids in on the act with Marshmallow Snowmen. You prepare the pan of marshmallow candy and set out the decorations. Then watch to see what manner of little creature takes shape. Here, our frosty friend sports chocolate chip eyes, a candy corn nose, and a cherry-sliver mouth. Additional trims, edible and otherwise, make up his attire.

mixture stand at room temperature at least 12 hours.

Loosen edges of marshmallow candy, using a sharp knife, and invert onto wax paper. Cut one-third of candy into 1½-inch circles, another third into 1¾-inch circles, and remaining third into 2-inch circles. Lightly dip each marshmallow circle in warm water and roll in flaked coconut. Assemble one of each size marshmallow on a wooden pick to form each snowman. Decorate snowmen with assorted candies and cherries. Store in airtight containers. Yield: 14 snowmen.

123

CINNAMON-SWIRL SWEET ROLLS

1 package dry yeast
½ cup plus 1 teaspoon sugar, divided
2 cups warm water (105° to 115°)
¾ cup shortening
1 egg, beaten
1 teaspoon salt
6 cups bread flour, divided
¼ cup plus 2 tablespoons butter or
  margarine, melted
2 teaspoons ground cinnamon
1 (8½-ounce) package red cinnamon
  candies, crushed or ground
1 cup finely chopped almonds, toasted
Glaze (recipe follows)
Candied red and green cherries
  (optional)
Silver décors (optional)

Dissolve yeast and 1 teaspoon sugar in warm water in a large bowl; let stand 5 minutes. Add remaining ½ cup sugar, shortening, egg, salt, and 3 cups flour; beat at low speed of an electric mixer until blended. Stir in enough of remaining 3 cups flour to make a soft dough.

Turn dough out onto a lightly floured surface; knead until smooth and elastic (8 to 10 minutes). Place dough in a large greased bowl, turning to grease top. Cover and let rise in a warm place (85°), free from drafts, 1 hour or until doubled in bulk.

Punch dough down and turn out onto a lightly floured surface; knead 4 or 5 times. Divide dough in half. Roll each half into a 24- x 8-inch rectangle. Combine butter and cinnamon, stirring until blended; brush over rectangles. Sprinkle cinnamon candy and almonds evenly over butter mixture, leaving a ½-inch margin around edges.

Tightly roll up each rectangle, jellyroll fashion, beginning at long sides; pinch edges together to seal. Cut rolls into ½-inch slices; place slices, cut side down, in 6 greased and wax paper-lined 8½-inch square baking pans. Cover and let rise in a warm place (85°), free from drafts, 1 hour or until doubled in bulk. Bake at 400° for 12 minutes or until rolls are lightly browned. Remove from oven and let cool. Remove from pans; remove and discard wax paper. Place each batch of sweet rolls on a wire rack; drizzle with glaze and garnish with candied cherries and silver décors, if desired. Yield: 8 dozen.

Glaze:
4 cups sifted powdered sugar
¼ cup plus 2 tablespoons half-and-half
½ teaspoon almond extract
⅛ teaspoon salt

Combine sugar, half-and-half, almond extract, and salt in a medium saucepan; cook over low heat until smooth, stirring frequently. Remove from heat and cool slightly. Yield: about 1½ cups.

ZESTY GOURMET MUSTARD

¾ cup white wine vinegar
⅓ cup dry mustard
⅓ cup sugar
2 tablespoons all-purpose flour
½ teaspoon salt
¾ cup half-and-half
1 egg, beaten

Combine vinegar and mustard in top of a non-aluminum double boiler (do not stir). Cover and let stand at room temperature at least 8 hours.

Combine sugar, flour, and salt; gradually add to mustard mixture, stirring well with a wire whisk. Blend in half-and-half. Bring water to a boil; reduce heat and cook, stirring constantly, until slightly thickened. Gradually stir about one-fourth of hot mustard mixture into egg; quickly add to remaining hot mustard mixture, stirring constantly with a wire whisk. Continue to cook over simmering water, stirring constantly, until smooth and thickened. Remove from heat; cool and spoon into half-pint jars or airtight containers. Store in refrigerator. Stir well before serving. Yield: 2 half pints.

EASY SWEET-AND-SOUR SAUCE

¾ cup vinegar
⅔ cup firmly packed brown sugar
¼ cup plus 2 tablespoons orange juice
¼ cup unsweetened pineapple juice
¼ cup tomato paste
¼ teaspoon salt
⅛ teaspoon onion juice
1 tablespoon plus 1½ teaspoons
  cornstarch

Combine all ingredients, except cornstarch, in a medium saucepan, stirring with a wire whisk until blended. Remove ½ cup juice mixture and combine with cornstarch; stir until blended and set aside.

Cook juice mixture over medium-high heat until bubbly. Stir in cornstarch mixture; cook over medium-high heat, stirring constantly with a wire whisk, until smooth and thickened. Remove from heat; cool and spoon into half-pint jars or airtight containers. Store in refrigerator. Stir well before serving. Yield: 2 half pints.

HOLIDAY TEA BAGS

3 tablespoons tea leaves, divided
6 (3½-inch) sticks cinnamon, crushed
  and divided
Grated rind of 1 orange, divided
128 red cinnamon candies, divided
24 whole allspice, divided
16 whole cloves, divided

Place about 1½ teaspoons tea leaves and one-eighth each of crushed cinnamon and orange rind on a 7-inch, double-layer square of cheesecloth. Add 16 cinnamon candies, 3 whole allspice, and 2 whole cloves; tie securely with unwaxed dental floss or kite string. Attach a decorative tag to end of string, if desired. Repeat procedure to assemble 7 additional tea bags. Yield: 8 servings.

Directions for gift card: To serve, pour 1 cup boiling water over each tea bag; cover and let stand 5 minutes. Discard tea bags and garnish each serving with a lemon slice, if desired.

ITALIAN-SEASONED DRESSING AND CROUTONS

1 cup white wine vinegar
½ cup sugar
2 teaspoons cornstarch
2 teaspoons dried whole oregano
1½ teaspoons dried whole basil
1½ teaspoons dried whole marjoram
1 cup olive oil
Favorite Herbed Croutons (recipe
  follows)

Combine first 3 ingredients in a medium saucepan, stirring well. Cook over medium heat, stirring frequently, until slightly thickened. Remove from heat; cool slightly.

Pour mixture into container of an electric blender and add herbs; cover and process until combined. Turn blender to low speed; add oil in a slow, steady stream. Turn blender to high speed; process until mixture starts to thicken. Cover and refrigerate until thoroughly chilled. Shake well and serve over salad greens, topped with Favorite Herbed Croutons. Yield: 2 cups.

Favorite Herbed Croutons:
1 cup butter or margarine, melted
1 tablespoon plus 1 teaspoon grated
  Parmesan cheese
1 tablespoon plus 1 teaspoon parsley
  flakes
1 tablespoon garlic powder
¼ teaspoon celery salt
1 (¾-pound) unsliced loaf day-old rye
  bread, cut into ¾-inch cubes

Combine first 5 ingredients, stirring well; pour over bread cubes and toss gently to coat. Place in a single layer on an ungreased baking sheet. Bake at 300° for 25 minutes, stirring occasionally. Drain on paper towels. Store in an airtight container. Yield: 8 cups.

RASPBERRY TRUFFLES

¼ cup whipping cream
1 (6-ounce) package semisweet
 chocolate morsels
2 tablespoons Chambord or other
 raspberry-flavored liqueur
¼ cup butter, softened
About ¼ cup chocolate-flavored décors
About ¼ cup multicolored décors

Place cream in a small saucepan; cook over medium heat, stirring constantly, until mixture is reduced to 2 tablespoons. Add morsels and liqueur. Reduce heat to low; cook, stirring constantly, until morsels melt. Add butter; beat with a wire whisk until melted. Remove from heat; cover and refrigerate 1 hour.

Shape mixture into 1-inch balls; cover and refrigerate 1 hour. Roll truffles in chocolate-flavored décors, and then in multicolored décors. Refrigerate in an airtight container. Yield: about 2½ dozen.

CANDY-COATED PRETZEL WREATHS

1½ pounds vanilla-flavored almond
 bark
1 (9-ounce) package mini-pretzel
 twists
1 (6-ounce) package semisweet
 chocolate morsels (optional)
Red cinnamon candies (optional)
Candied green cherries (optional)

Place almond bark in top of a double boiler; bring water to a boil. Reduce heat to low; cook until almond bark melts. Dip 10 pretzels, 5 at a time, in almond bark. Remove pretzels, one at a time, with a fork,

---

Right: Gather together all the materials—tissue and cellophane, pressed glassware and tins, baskets and boxes. Then pack up these one-of-a-kind gifts from the kitchen. Shown clockwise from back are Italian-Seasoned Dressing and Croutons, Zesty Gourmet Mustard, Easy Sweet-and-Sour Sauce, Holiday Tea Bags, Candy-Coated Pretzel Wreaths, and Cinnamon-Swirl Sweet Rolls.

126

allowing excess almond bark to drain back into pan; place on a wax paper-lined baking sheet. Working on baking sheet, immediately arrange 5 coated pretzels, twisted edge out, in a circle with sides joining to form bottom layer of wreath. Quickly repeat process, making a second layer with remaining 5 coated pretzels. Repeat entire procedure to assemble about 9 additional pretzel wreaths. Allow coated wreaths to harden.

Carefully remove wreaths from wax paper; transfer to wire racks. Using a small brush, spread remaining almond bark over wreaths to provide a thicker coating. Allow almond bark to harden.

If desired, place chocolate in top of a double boiler; bring water to a boil. Reduce heat to low; cook until chocolate melts. Drizzle chocolate over wreaths; allow chocolate to harden. Carefully remove wreaths from racks and garnish with cinnamon

candies and cherries, if desired (attach with melted almond bark or chocolate, if needed). Yield: about 10 wreaths.

SOUR CREAM FESTIVE FUDGE
3¼ cups sugar
¾ cup commercial sour cream
¼ cup plus 2 tablespoons milk
2 tablespoons light corn syrup
¼ teaspoon salt
3 tablespoons butter or margarine
¾ teaspoon almond extract
1 cup chopped pecans
½ cup chopped candied red cherries
½ cup chopped candied green cherries

Combine first 5 ingredients in a medium Dutch oven, stirring until blended. Bring to a boil; cook over medium heat, stirring frequently, until sugar dissolves. Wash off sugar crystals from sides of pan, using a

brush dipped in cold water. Continue to cook over medium heat, without stirring, until mixture reaches soft ball stage (236°). Remove from heat and add butter (do not stir); let stand 15 minutes. Add almond extract; beat with a wooden spoon 2 minutes or just until mixture begins to thicken. Quickly stir in pecans and cherries; beat with wooden spoon until combined.

Working rapidly, spoon mixture into a buttered 8-inch square pan. Mark top of warm fudge into 1⅓-inch squares, using a sharp knife. Cool completely before cutting into squares. Yield: 3 dozen.

CHOCOLATE MARZIPAN CONFECTIONS
¾ cup finely chopped walnuts
3 tablespoons bourbon, divided
2 (8-ounce) cans almond paste, crumbled
Powdered sugar
1 (6-ounce) package semisweet chocolate morsels
1½ teaspoons shortening
About 4 dozen small walnut halves

Combine chopped walnuts and 2 tablespoons bourbon in a medium bowl, stirring well. Cover and let stand at room temperature at least 8 hours. Add remaining 1 tablespoon bourbon and almond paste to chopped walnuts; stir until combined (knead mixture with hands, if necessary).

Roll mixture out to ½-inch thickness on a surface lightly sifted with powdered sugar. Using a sharp knife, cut mixture into 1½-inch-long trapezoidal shapes with a 1-inch base. Cover and refrigerate 1 hour.

Combine chocolate and shortening in top of a double boiler; bring water to a boil. Reduce heat to low; cook, stirring constantly, until melted. Dip each piece of candy in chocolate, allowing excess to drain back into pan. Place candy on wax paper; top each piece with a walnut half. Allow chocolate to harden. Refrigerate in an airtight container. Yield: about 4 dozen.

Patterns

Index

Santa Lives Here

**Instructions are on page 48.
Patterns are full-size.**

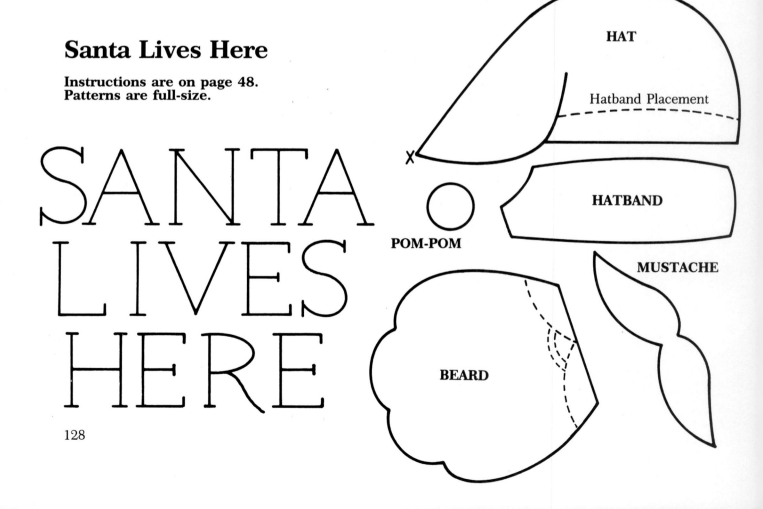

128

Clowning Around

Instructions are on page 81.
Patterns are full-size.
Patterns include ¼″ seam allowance.

Gather.

Center

LEGS
Cut 1.

Gather.

Place on fold.

Gather.

Center

ARMS
Cut 1.

Gather.

HAT
Cut 1; reverse
and cut 1.

Attach head here.

HEAD
Cut 2.

TREE
Green

Wearable Art

Instructions are on page 82.
Patterns are full-size.

PAINTED SWEATSHIRT

Make a template from pattern and stencil on shirt.
Sponge-paint tree green and trunk brown.

TRUNK
Brown

129

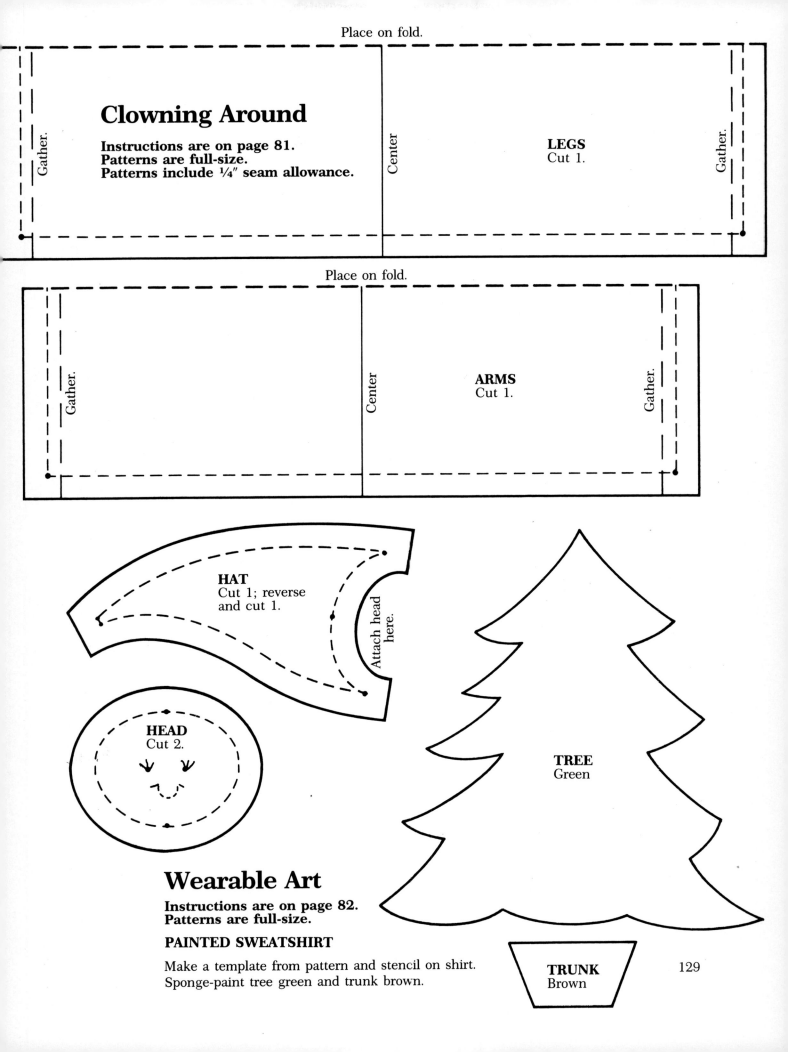

Storybook Bear: A Keepsake Ornament

Instructions are on page 72.
Patterns are full-size.

Ski Bunny Takes to the Slopes

Instructions are on page 60.
Patterns are full-size.

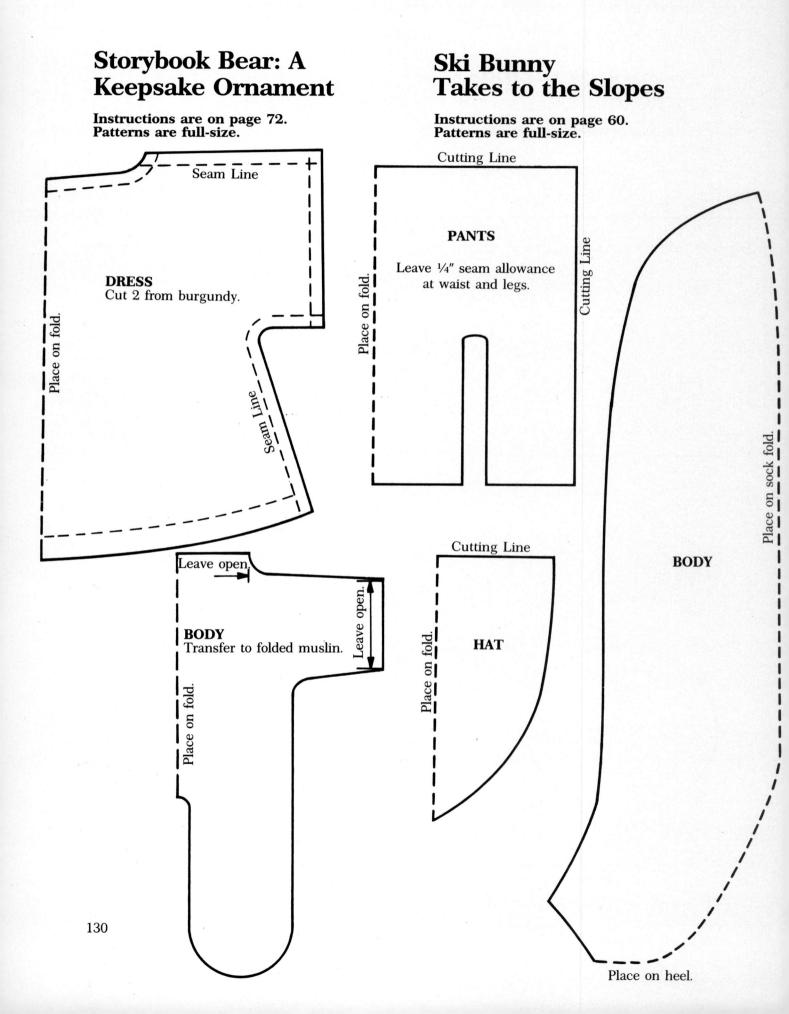

Seam Line

DRESS
Cut 2 from burgundy.

Place on fold.

Seam Line

Leave open.

BODY
Transfer to folded muslin.

Leave open.

Place on fold.

Cutting Line

PANTS

Leave ¼" seam allowance
at waist and legs.

Place on fold.

Cutting Line

Cutting Line

HAT

Place on fold.

BODY

Place on sock fold.

Place on heel.

130

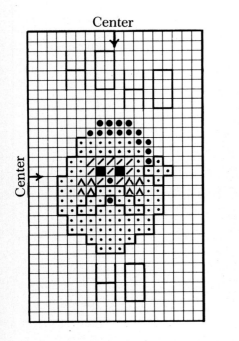

Center

Gild Your Tree with Golden Sleds
Instructions are on page 66.

Color Key
Note: Numbers are for DMC floss.

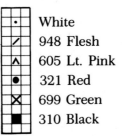

·	White
/	948 Flesh
∧	605 Lt. Pink
●	321 Red
✕	699 Green
■	310 Black

Use 3 strands of floss for all cross-stitching.

Use 1 strand of black for backstitching.

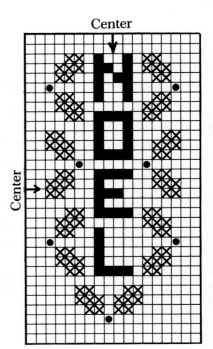

Center

Center

A Circle of Puppy Love

Instructions are on page 49.
Patterns are full-size.
Add ¼″ seam allowance.

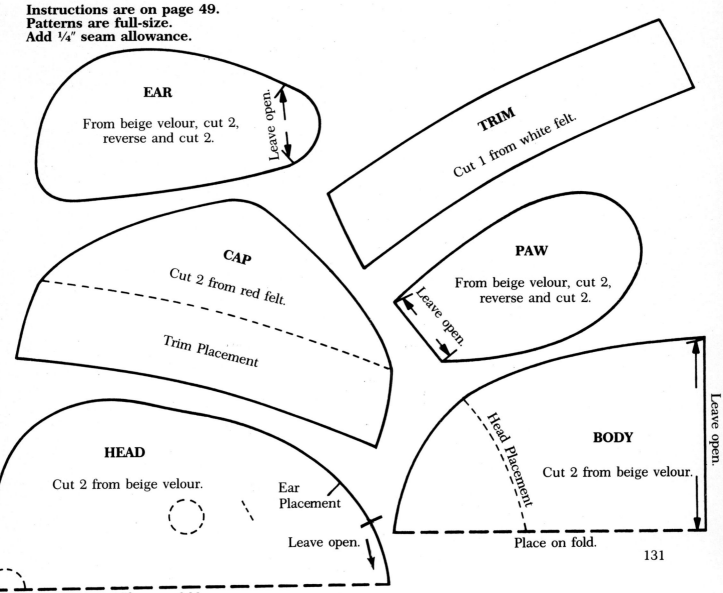

EAR

From beige velour, cut 2, reverse and cut 2.

Leave open.

TRIM

Cut 1 from white felt.

CAP

Cut 2 from red felt.

Trim Placement

PAW

From beige velour, cut 2, reverse and cut 2.

Leave open.

Head Placement

BODY

Cut 2 from beige velour.

Leave open.

HEAD

Cut 2 from beige velour.

Ear Placement

Leave open.

Place on fold.

Place on fold.

131

Lambs Parade on a Patchwork Stocking

**Instructions are on page 46.
Patterns include a ¼″ seam allowance.**

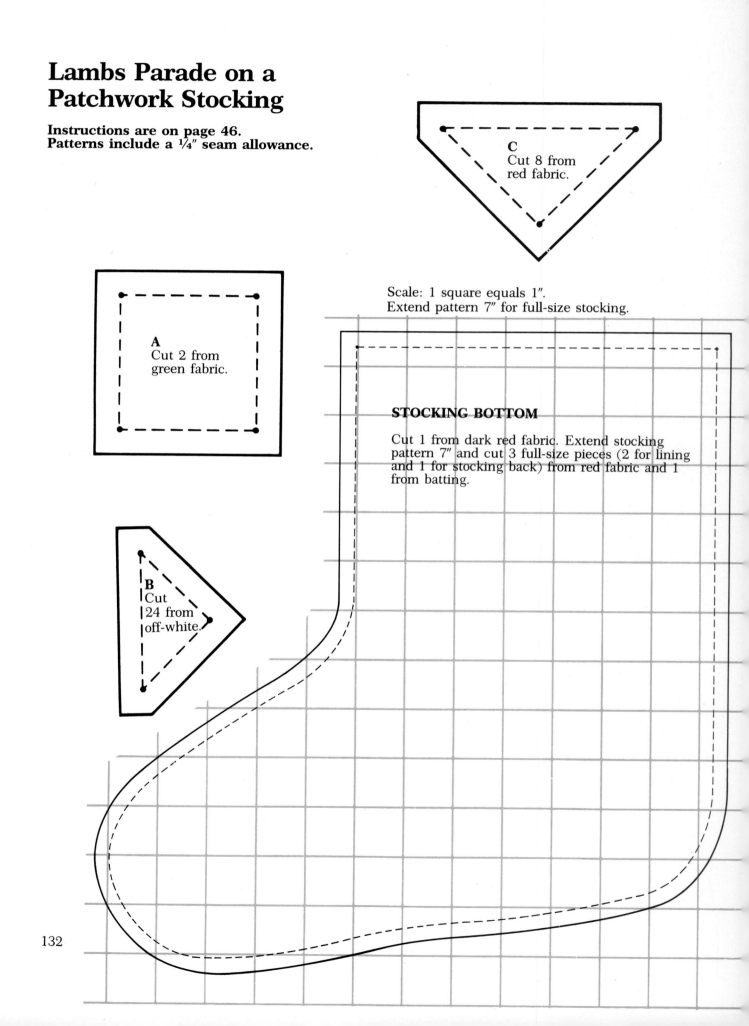

C
Cut 8 from
red fabric.

A
Cut 2 from
green fabric.

B
Cut
24 from
off-white.

Scale: 1 square equals 1″.
Extend pattern 7″ for full-size stocking.

STOCKING BOTTOM

Cut 1 from dark red fabric. Extend stocking
pattern 7″ and cut 3 full-size pieces (2 for lining
and 1 for stocking back) from red fabric and 1
from batting.

CROSS-STITCH CHART FOR PIECE D

Center

Center

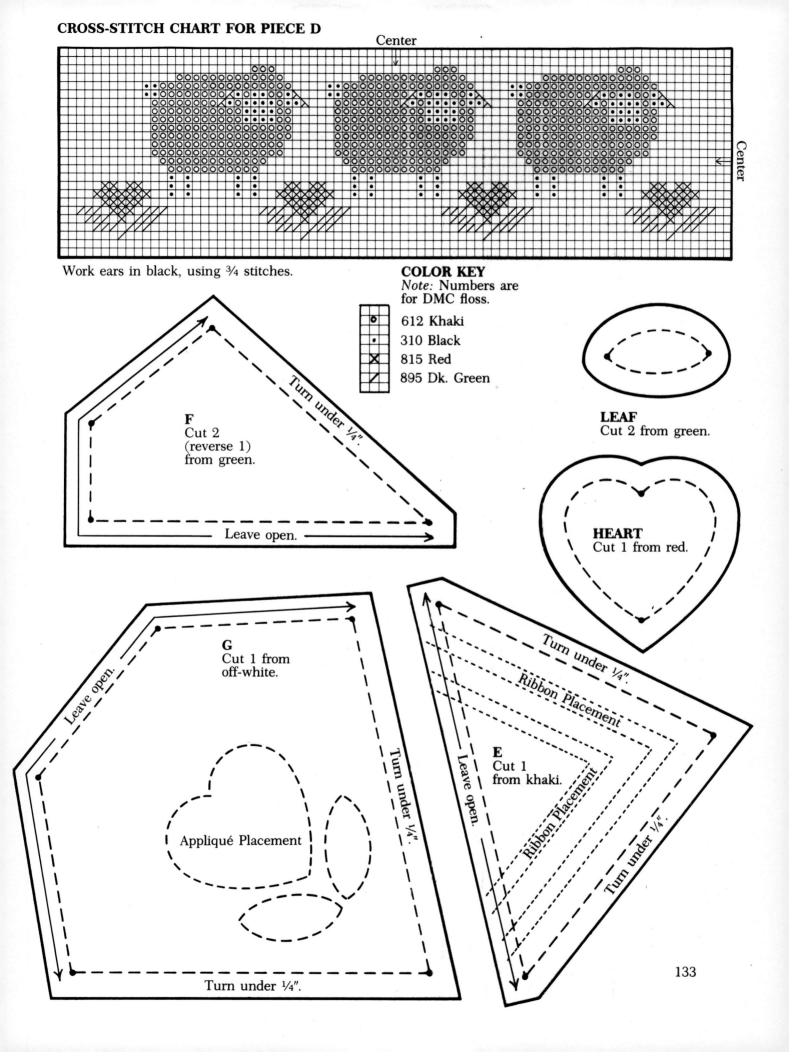

Work ears in black, using ¾ stitches.

COLOR KEY
Note: Numbers are for DMC floss.

⊙	612 Khaki
•	310 Black
✕	815 Red
╱	895 Dk. Green

F
Cut 2
(reverse 1)
from green.

Turn under ¼".

Leave open.

LEAF
Cut 2 from green.

HEART
Cut 1 from red.

G
Cut 1 from off-white.

Leave open.

Turn under ¼".

Appliqué Placement

Turn under ¼".

Turn under ¼".

Ribbon Placement

E
Cut 1
from khaki.

Leave open.

Ribbon Placement

Turn under ¼".

A Basket of Christmas Tulips

Instructions are on page 38.
Patterns include ¼″ seam allowance.

For Pattern B, cut
10 from green pindot.

For Pattern C, cut 4
from cream fabric.

For Pattern D, cut 1 from paper,
cut 2 from batting, and cut
3 from green pindot.

For Tulip, cut all 3
pieces to make 1 template.

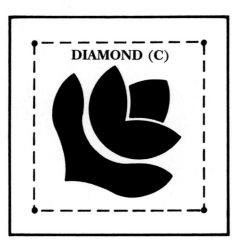

DIAMOND (C)

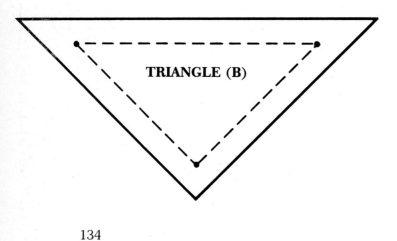

TRIANGLE (B)

BASKET PATTERN (D)

Scale: 1 square
equals 1″.

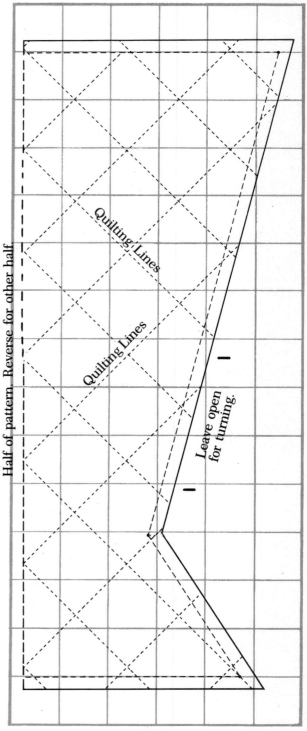

Quilting Lines

Quilting Lines

Half of pattern. Reverse for other half

Leave open for turning.

A Jolly Reindeer Cookie Carrier

**Instructions are on page 50.
Patterns are full-size.**

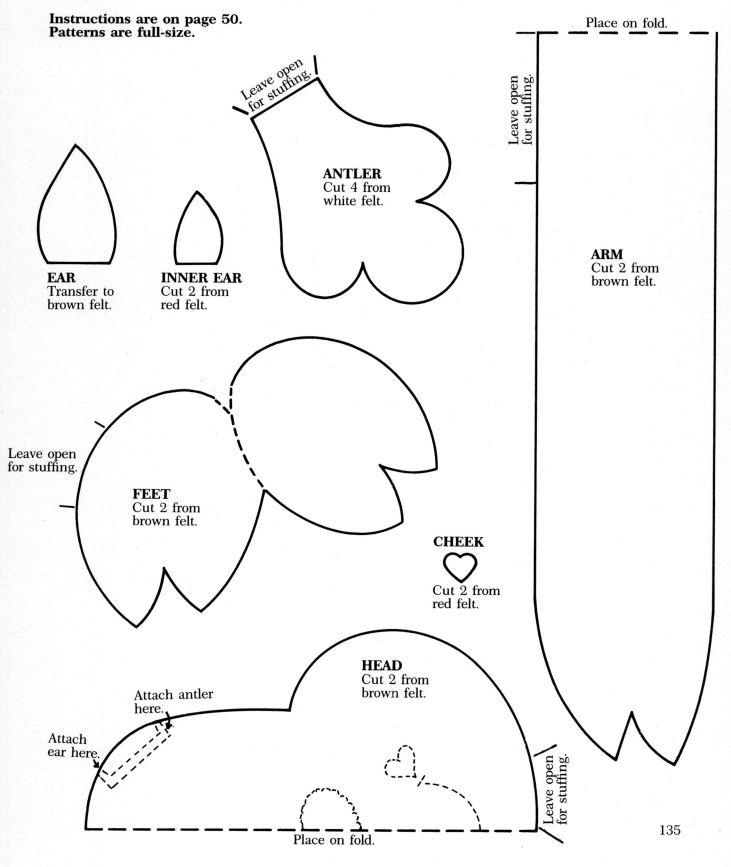

Place on fold.

Leave open
for stuffing.

Leave open
for stuffing.

ANTLER
Cut 4 from
white felt.

ARM
Cut 2 from
brown felt.

EAR
Transfer to
brown felt.

INNER EAR
Cut 2 from
red felt.

Leave open
for stuffing.

FEET
Cut 2 from
brown felt.

CHEEK
Cut 2 from
red felt.

Attach antler
here.

Attach
ear here.

HEAD
Cut 2 from
brown felt.

Leave open
for stuffing.

Place on fold.

135

Decorate Your Lawn with Forest Friends

Instructions are on page 44.
Scale: 1 square equals 1″.

Christmas Eve Nightie

Instructions are on page 76.
Patterns are full-size.

For Highlight, satin-stitch a ¼″ curved white line.

For Trunk, cut a 2″ x 1¾″ piece from Christmas miniprint.

Attach stem here.

HIGHLIGHT

APPLE
Cut 12 from red pindot.

LEAF
Cut 12 from green plaid.

STEM
Cut 12 from brown pindot.

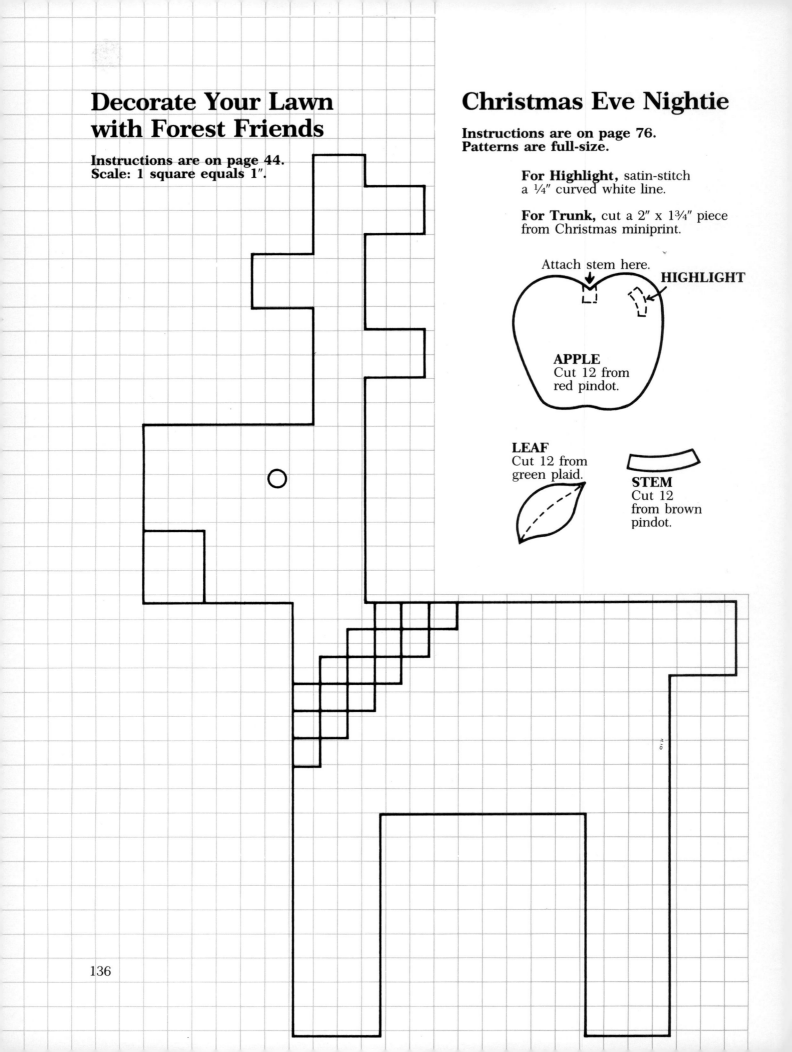

136

Merry Mouse Card Holder

Instructions are on page 51.

Stitch border in green.

Weave print ribbon over package, entering at top X, exiting at X above hands, entering again at X below hands, and exiting at bottom X. Glue ribbon bow at top X.

Color Key

⊙	Red
·	Pink
▮	Dark Green
╲	Gray
╱	Dk. Red
✕	Green
☐	White
■	Black

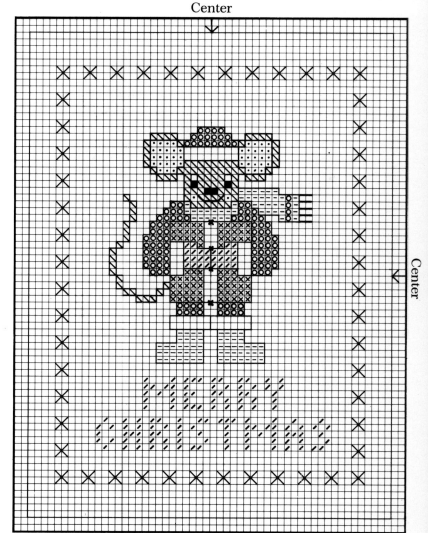

Center

Center

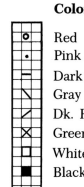

Decorate Your Lawn with Forest Friends

Instructions are on page 44.
Pattern for cardinal is full-size.

Hole for Hanger

A Handy Mitt

Instructions are on page 93.
Patterns include a ⅛″ seam allowance.

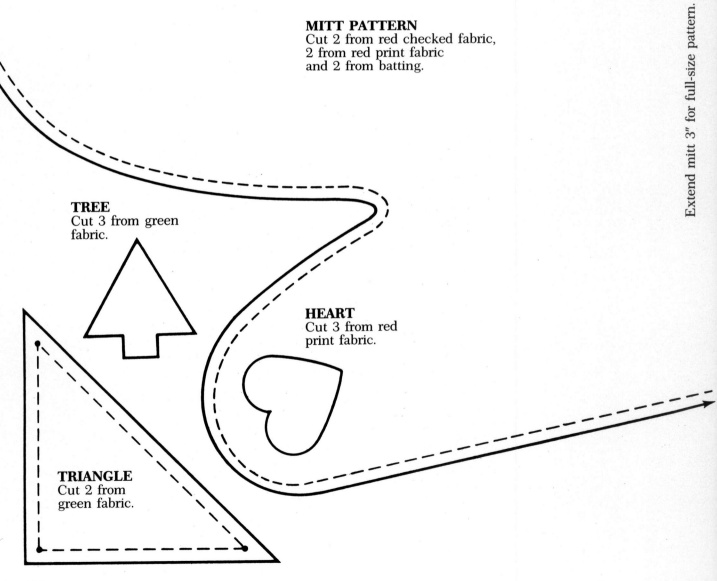

MITT PATTERN
Cut 2 from red checked fabric,
2 from red print fabric
and 2 from batting.

TREE
Cut 3 from green
fabric.

HEART
Cut 3 from red
print fabric.

TRIANGLE
Cut 2 from
green fabric.

Extend mitt 3″ for full-size pattern.

Cross-Stitch Sampler with a Special Verse

Instructions are on page 34.

Use 1 strand of floss for all cross-stitching.

Color Key

Note: Numbers are for DMC floss.

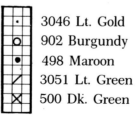

·	3046 Lt. Gold
o	902 Burgundy
●	498 Maroon
/	3051 Lt. Green
X	500 Dk. Green

Potpourri and Paper: a Cross-Stitch Sachet

Instructions are on page 92.

Color Key
Note: Numbers are for DMC floss.

☒	3685 Dk. Rose
☒	3687 Med. Dk. Rose
☒	3688 Med. Lt. Rose
☒	3689 Lt. Rose
○	500 Dk. Green
◿	501 Med. Green
■	503 Lt. Green
═	730 Olive Green
◤	793 Med. Blue
◤	3047 Cream

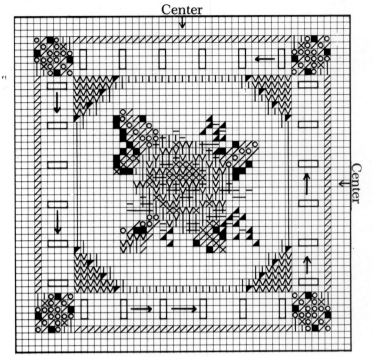

Cut slots as indicated for ribbon insert.
Weave ribbon in direction of arrows.
Use 3 strands of floss to cross-stitch.

Simply Elegant Greetings

**Instructions are on page 35.
Patterns are full-size.**

Wearable Art

Instructions are on page 82.
Patterns are full-size.

SHRINK-ART SWEATSHIRT

For Sheep, paint face, ear, tail, and legs black. Paint wavy ground lines black.

For Snowman, paint details black.

For House, paint chimney smoke gray, with a touch of black. Work blue into wet white paint to highlight sidewalk and snow on ground.

For Balls, paint top gold. Paint balls any color desired. Use dotted lines to shade as described in instructions.

For Duck, paint wavy water lines blue. Paint tail gold and eye black.

Ornamental Hexagons Banded with Color

Instructions are on page 67.
Pattern is full-size.

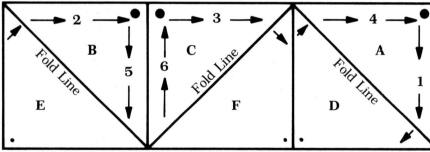

Cut 1 from cardboard. With craft knife, lightly score on fold lines.

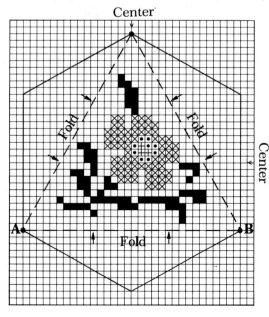

Tapestry Flower Ornaments

Instructions are on page 42.

Color Key

 Main Color

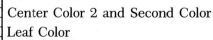 Center Color 1

Center Color 2 and Second Color

Leaf Color

Cut 8 hexagons from perforated paper.

Lightly score along fold lines.

Reverse Main Color and Center Color 2 for 4 of the 8 hexagons.

Use 3 strands of floss to work design.

141

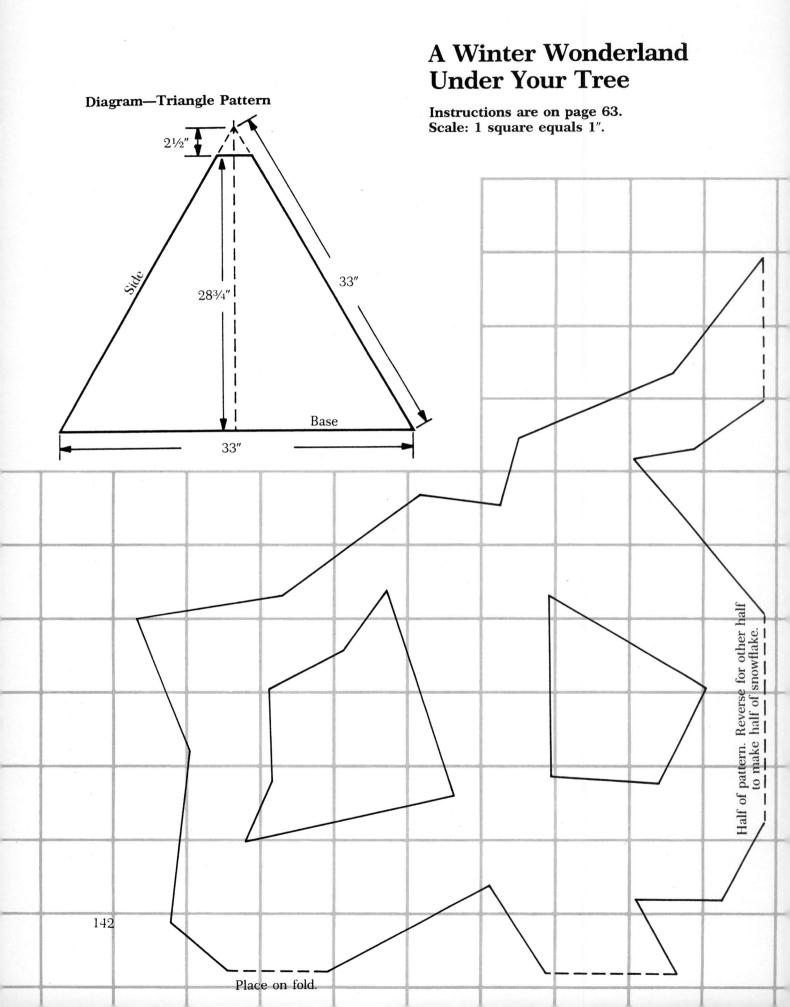

Diagram—Triangle Pattern

2½″

Side

28¾″

33″

Base

33″

A Winter Wonderland
Under Your Tree

Instructions are on page 63.
Scale: 1 square equals 1″.

Half of pattern. Reverse for other half to make half of snowflake.

142

Place on fold.

A Jolly Pair

Instructions are on page 70.
Patterns are full-size.

For Kris Kringle's belt, cut a strip ½″ x 4¾″ from black felt, pin to body front, trim sides to match, and appliqué in place.

For each doll's arms, cut 2 (3½″ x 2⅜″) pieces from miniprint and fold in half, short ends together.

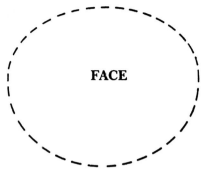

FACE

Refer to photo to draw faces.

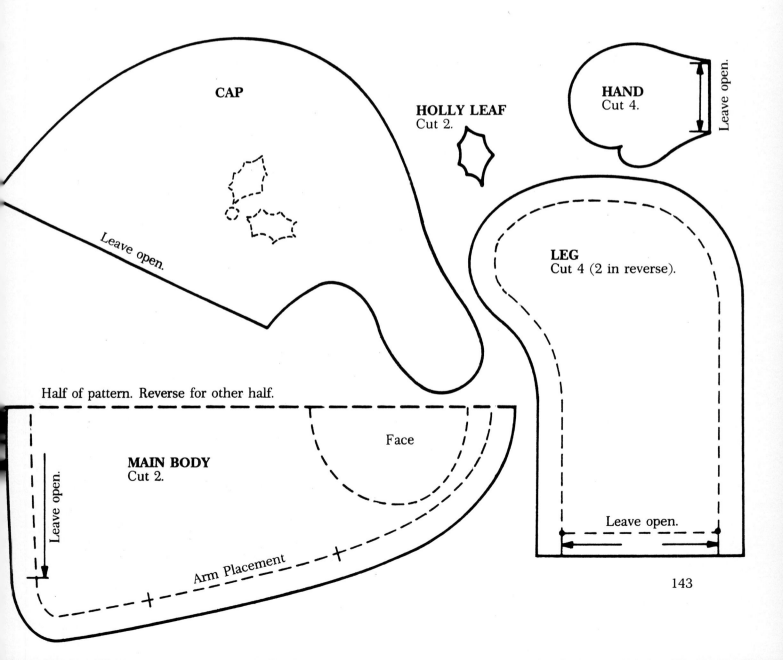

CAP

Leave open.

HOLLY LEAF
Cut 2.

HAND
Cut 4.

Leave open.

LEG
Cut 4 (2 in reverse).

Half of pattern. Reverse for other half.

Face

MAIN BODY
Cut 2.

Leave open.

Arm Placement

Leave open.

143

Beaded Baubles

Instructions are on page 36.

Color Key

Emerald
Garnet
Gold

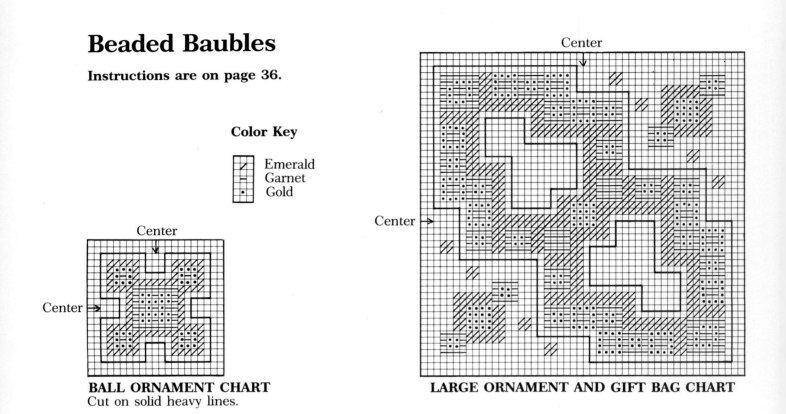

BALL ORNAMENT CHART
Cut on solid heavy lines.

LARGE ORNAMENT AND GIFT BAG CHART

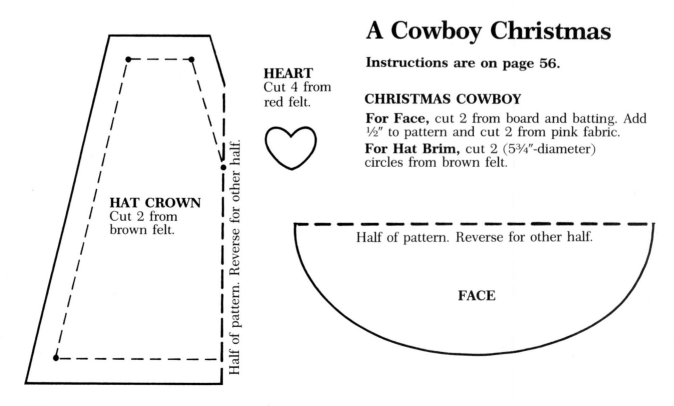

HAT CROWN
Cut 2 from
brown felt.

Half of pattern. Reverse for other half.

HEART
Cut 4 from
red felt.

A Cowboy Christmas

Instructions are on page 56.

CHRISTMAS COWBOY

For Face, cut 2 from board and batting. Add
½″ to pattern and cut 2 from pink fabric.
For Hat Brim, cut 2 (5¾″-diameter)
circles from brown felt.

Half of pattern. Reverse for other half.

FACE

Snowdrift Tree Skirt

Instructions are on page 52.
Pattern is full-size.
¼″ seam allowance is included.

Cut 28 from red miniprint.
Cut 14 from white print.

For Snowdrift Tree Skirt, hearts, leave open.

A Ruffled Wreath Made to Last

Instructions are on page 58.
Pattern is full-size.

Cut 2 from cardboard.
Add ⅜″ all around and cut 2 from fabric.

Paint dots on heart.
Pencil message in middle, paint in red, and place dots at beginnings and ends of letters.

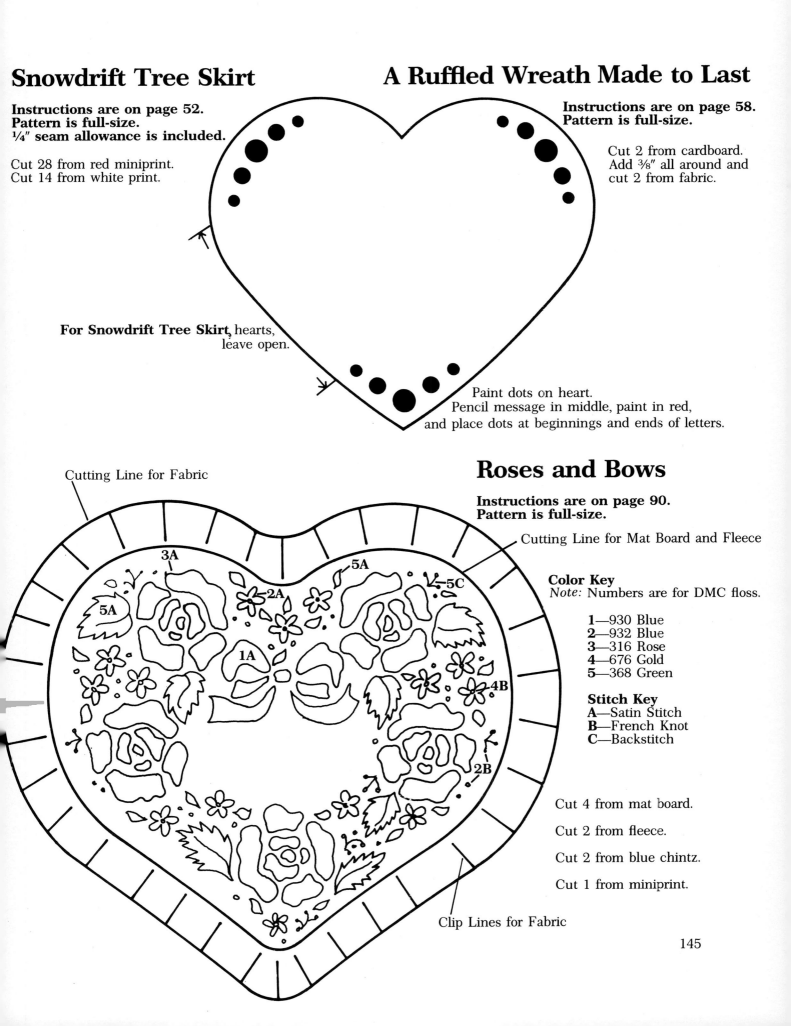

Cutting Line for Fabric

Roses and Bows

Instructions are on page 90.
Pattern is full-size.

Cutting Line for Mat Board and Fleece

Color Key
Note: Numbers are for DMC floss.

1—930 Blue
2—932 Blue
3—316 Rose
4—676 Gold
5—368 Green

Stitch Key
A—Satin Stitch
B—French Knot
C—Backstitch

Cut 4 from mat board.

Cut 2 from fleece.

Cut 2 from blue chintz.

Cut 1 from miniprint.

Clip Lines for Fabric

145

Swiss-Style Baby Bunting

**Instructions are on page 77.
Patterns are full-size.**

Heavy lines are appliqué lines, and thin lines
are painting lines.

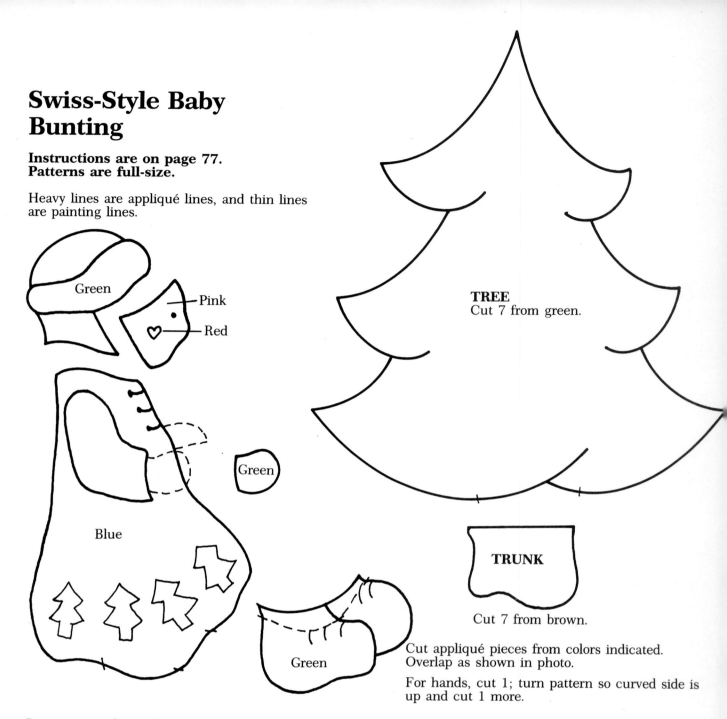

Green

Pink

Red

Green

Blue

Green

TREE
Cut 7 from green.

TRUNK

Cut 7 from brown.

Cut appliqué pieces from colors indicated.
Overlap as shown in photo.

For hands, cut 1; turn pattern so curved side is
up and cut 1 more.

Diagram—Appliqué Placement

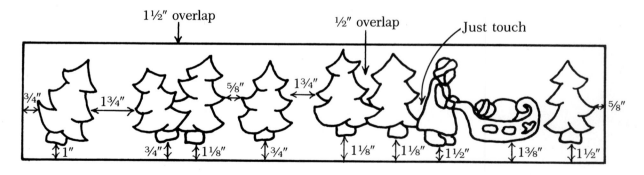

1½″ overlap

½″ overlap

Just touch

¾″

1¾″

5⁄8″

1¾″

1″

¾″

1⅛″

¾″

1⅛″

1⅛″

1½″

1⅜″

1½″

5⁄8″

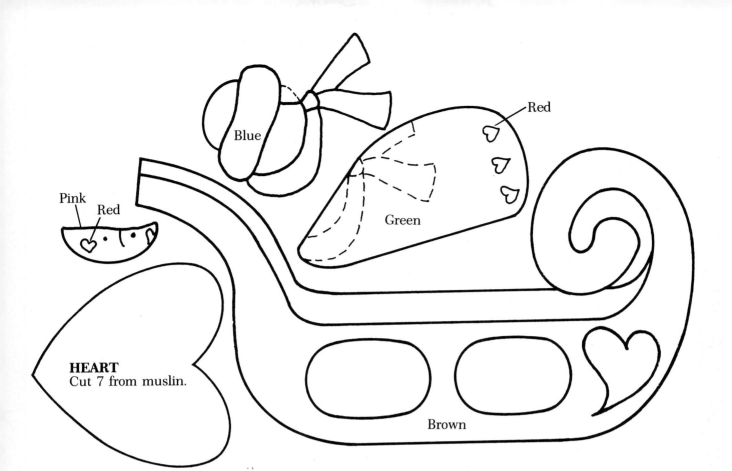

HEART
Cut 7 from muslin.

Pink

Red

Blue

Red

Green

Brown

Christmas Sweatshirt with Celestial Charm

Instructions are on page 85.

CROSS-STITCH CHART

Color Key
Note: All colors are for DMC floss.

·	3706 Pink
●	321 Christmas Red
o	503 Lt. Green
X	910 Dk. Green
I	950 Beige
—	676 Lt. Gold
/	783 Dk. Gold
\	725 Yellow

Make French knot eyes with 2 strands of black floss, or substitute a color if desired.

Backstitch lines with 2 strands of black. Backstitch letters with 3 strands of Christmas red.

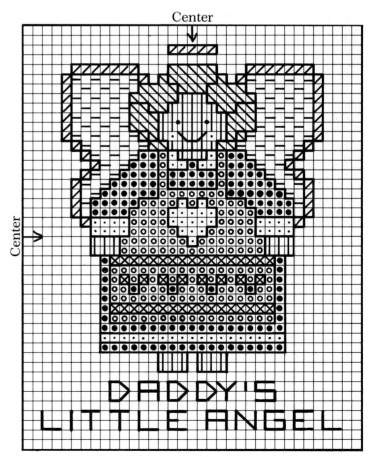

Center

Center

DADDY'S LITTLE ANGEL

147

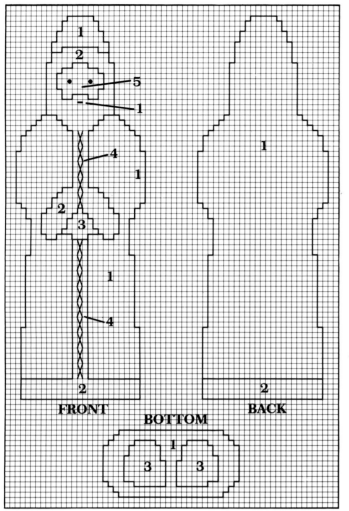

Knit St. Nick in the Nick of Time

Instructions are on page 45.

CHART FOR KNITTING

1—Red
2—White
3—Black
4—Green
5—Pink

A Cowboy Christmas

Instructions are on page 56.

ROCKING HORSE

For Horse Body and Legs, cut 1 each from board and batting. Add ¼″ to pattern pieces and cut 1 each from red fabric.

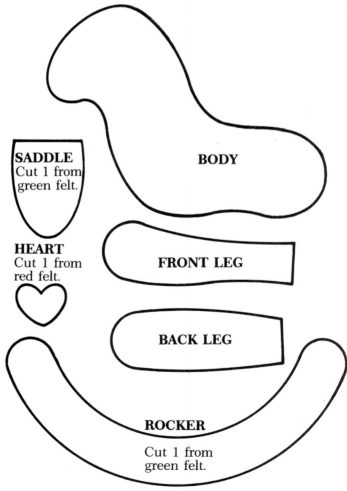

SADDLE
Cut 1 from green felt.

BODY

HEART
Cut 1 from red felt.

FRONT LEG

BACK LEG

ROCKER

Cut 1 from green felt.

148

Nordic-Inspired Design

Instructions are on page 88.
Pattern is full-size.

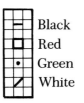

⊟	Black
▢	Red
⊡	Green
⊘	White

NORDIC TRAY

Draw a rectangle ⅜″ smaller on all sides than surface of tray. Center this line on short end, repeat design in each direction to fill width of tray, wrapping outside diamond border around sides (see photo). Repeat for other side. Center a tree in space between designs.

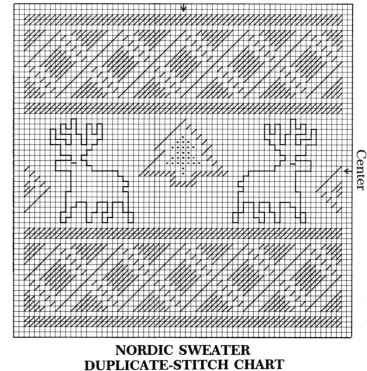

NORDIC SWEATER
DUPLICATE-STITCH CHART

Diagram—Duplicate-Stitch Embroidery

Begin at base of stitch to be covered. Sew under stitch above; then insert needle back into starting point.

149

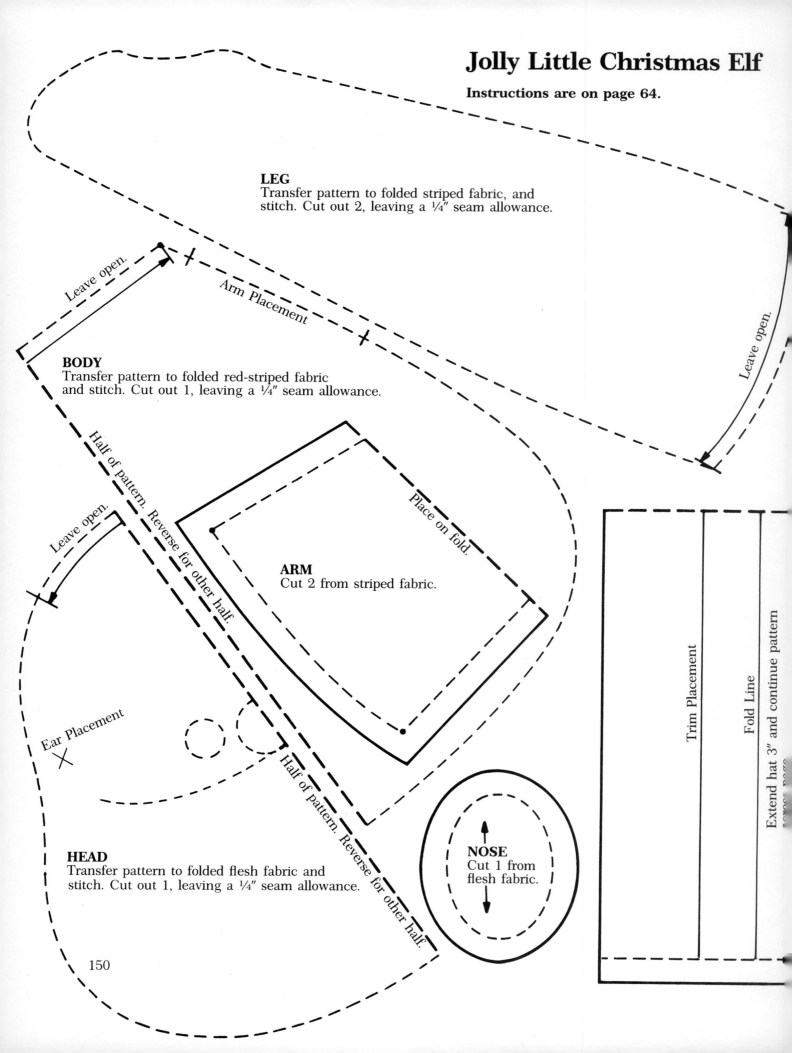

Jolly Little Christmas Elf

Instructions are on page 64.

LEG
Transfer pattern to folded striped fabric, and stitch. Cut out 2, leaving a ¼" seam allowance.

Leave open.

Arm Placement

BODY
Transfer pattern to folded red-striped fabric and stitch. Cut out 1, leaving a ¼" seam allowance.

Leave open.

Half of pattern. Reverse for other half.

Place on fold.

Leave open.

ARM
Cut 2 from striped fabric.

Ear Placement

Half of pattern. Reverse for other half.

HEAD
Transfer pattern to folded flesh fabric and stitch. Cut out 1, leaving a ¼" seam allowance.

NOSE
Cut 1 from flesh fabric.

Trim Placement

Fold Line

Extend hat 3" and continue pattern

150

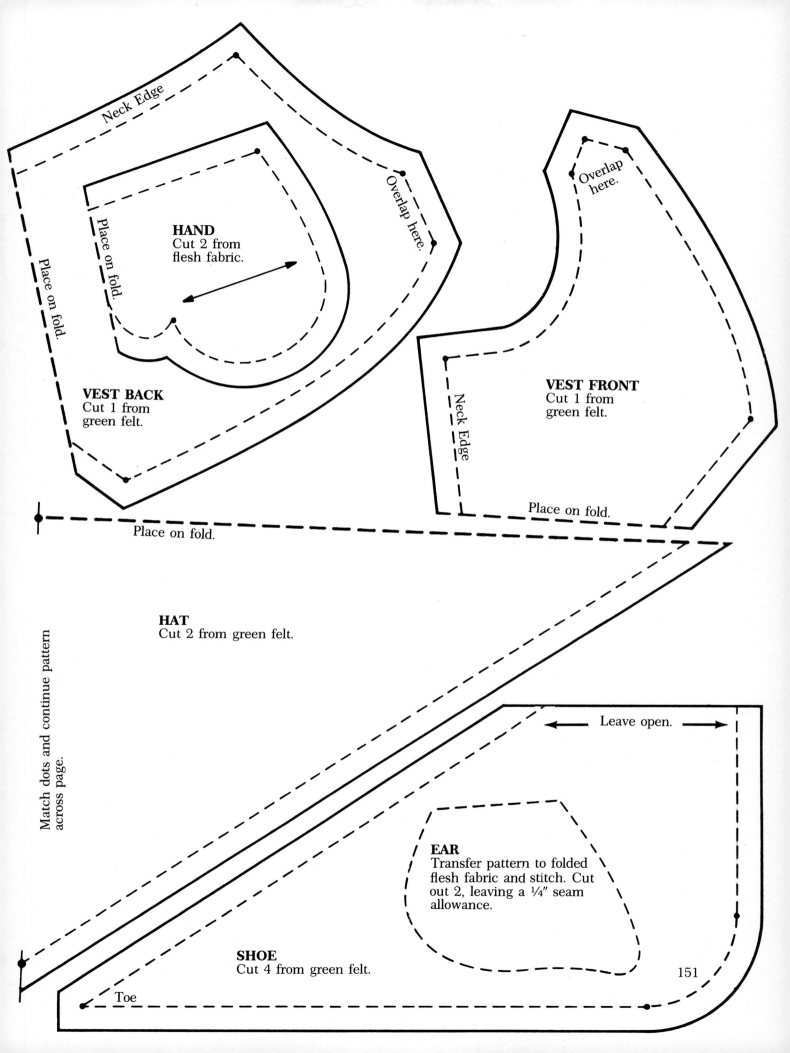

HAND
Cut 2 from
flesh fabric.

VEST BACK
Cut 1 from
green felt.

Neck Edge

Place on fold.

Place on fold.

Overlap here.

VEST FRONT
Cut 1 from
green felt.

Overlap here.

Neck Edge

Place on fold.

Place on fold.

HAT
Cut 2 from green felt.

Match dots and continue pattern across page.

Leave open.

EAR
Transfer pattern to folded
flesh fabric and stitch. Cut
out 2, leaving a ¼″ seam
allowance.

SHOE
Cut 4 from green felt.

Toe

151

A Cozy Cottage
Says Welcome

Instructions are on page 55.
Patterns are full-size.
Add ¼″ seam allowance to patterns.

Appliqué Placement
Overlap as shown in photo.

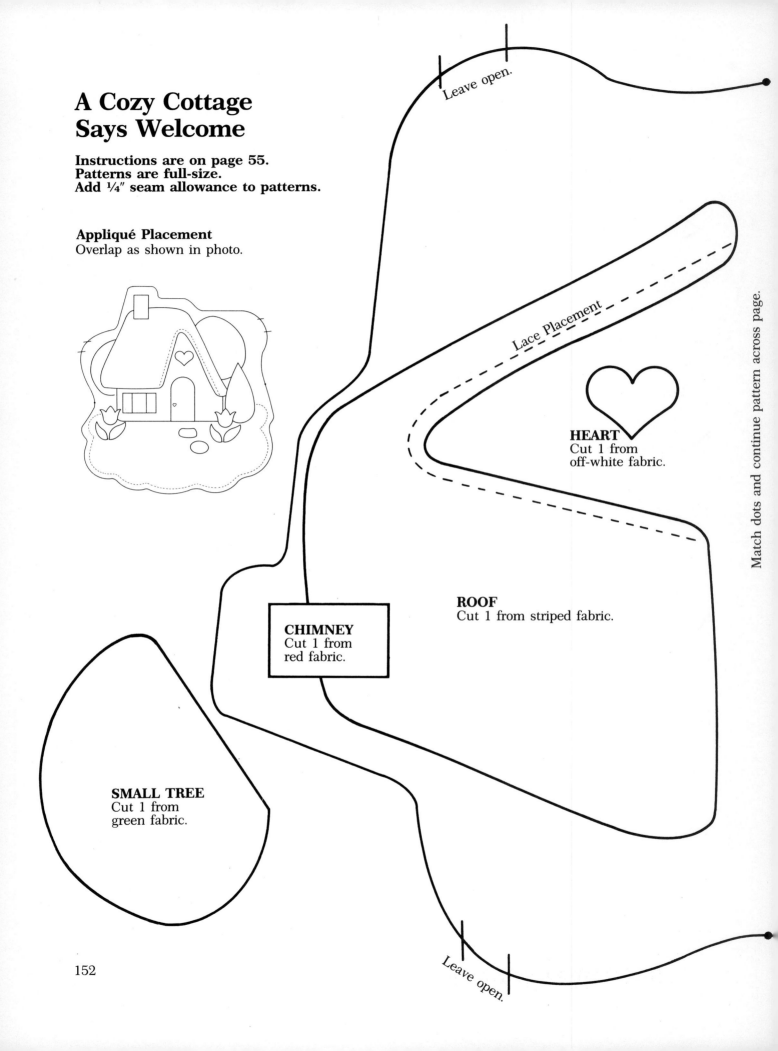

Leave open.

Lace Placement

HEART
Cut 1 from
off-white fabric.

ROOF
Cut 1 from striped fabric.

CHIMNEY
Cut 1 from
red fabric.

SMALL TREE
Cut 1 from
green fabric.

Leave open.

Match dots and continue pattern across page.

152

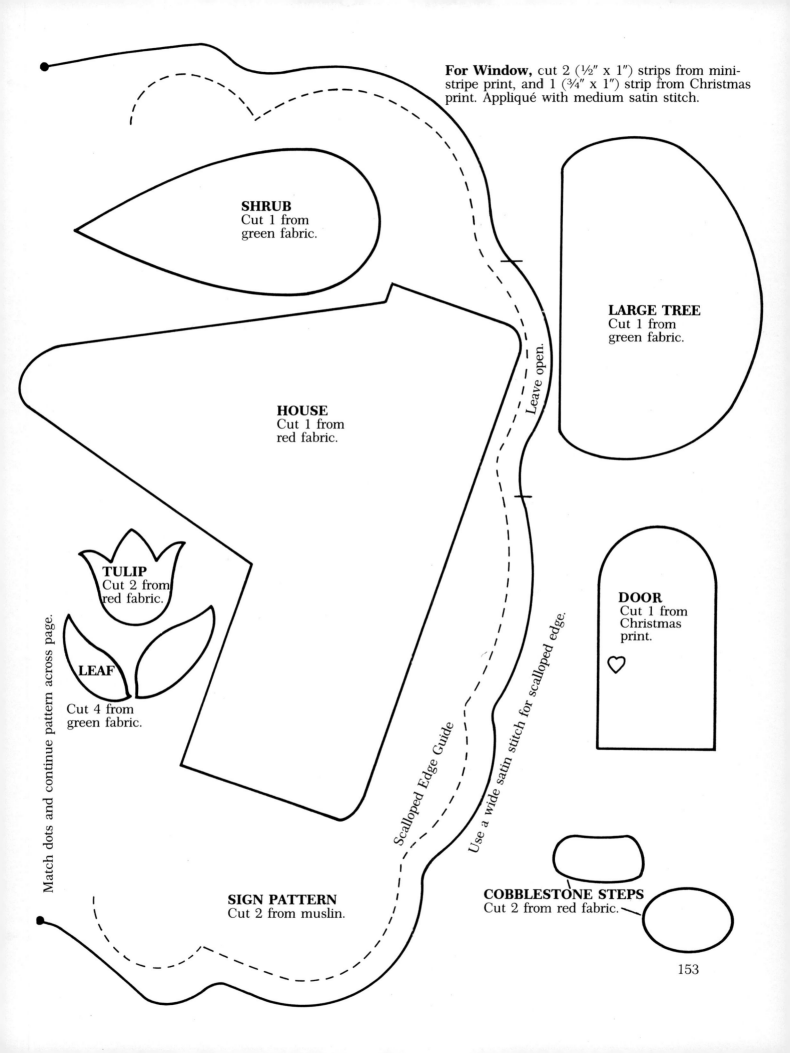

For Window, cut 2 (½″ x 1″) strips from mini-stripe print, and 1 (¾″ x 1″) strip from Christmas print. Appliqué with medium satin stitch.

SHRUB
Cut 1 from green fabric.

LARGE TREE
Cut 1 from green fabric.

Leave open.

HOUSE
Cut 1 from red fabric.

TULIP
Cut 2 from red fabric.

LEAF
Cut 4 from green fabric.

Match dots and continue pattern across page.

Scalloped Edge Guide

Use a wide satin stitch for scalloped edge.

DOOR
Cut 1 from Christmas print.

SIGN PATTERN
Cut 2 from muslin.

COBBLESTONE STEPS
Cut 2 from red fabric.

153

This Big Puppy Is a Cuddle-Buddy

Instructions are on page 87.
Scale: 1 square equals 1".

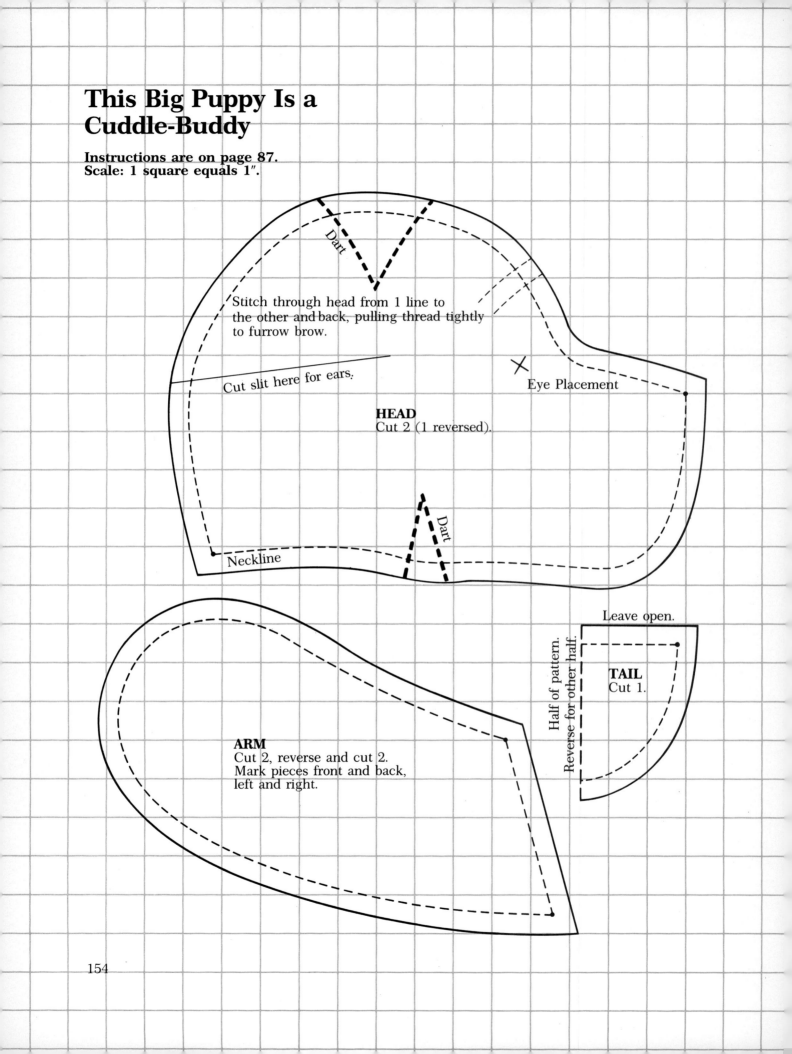

Dart

Stitch through head from 1 line to
the other and back, pulling thread tightly
to furrow brow.

Cut slit here for ears.

Eye Placement

HEAD
Cut 2 (1 reversed).

Dart

Neckline

Leave open.

Half of pattern.
Reverse for other half.

TAIL
Cut 1.

ARM
Cut 2, reverse and cut 2.
Mark pieces front and back,
left and right.

154

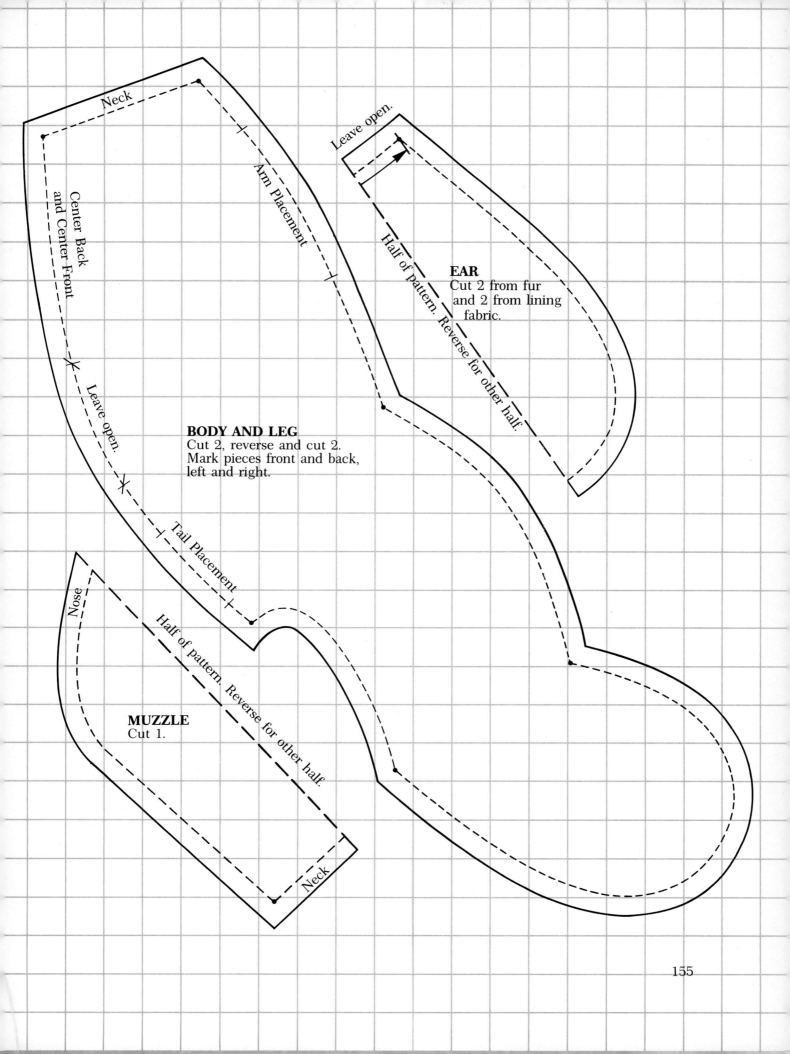

EAR
Cut 2 from fur
and 2 from lining
fabric.

Leave open.

Half of Pattern. Reverse for other half.

Neck

Center Back
and Center Front

Arm Placement

Leave open.

BODY AND LEG
Cut 2, reverse and cut 2.
Mark pieces front and back,
left and right.

Tail Placement

Nose

Half of pattern. Reverse for other half.

MUZZLE
Cut 1.

Neck

155

Contributors

DESIGNERS

Ellie Barber, tapestry flower ornaments, 42.

Barbara Blander and Joy Gerard, hexagonal yarn-wrapped ornaments, 67.

Amy Albert Bloom, reindeer and cardinal wooden lawn decorations, 44.

Diane C. Brakefield, embroidered needle case, 90.

Chere Brodsky, cowboy and horse ornaments, 56; "Dad" mug, 84.

Joanne Burkhart, clowns, 81.

Bea Crowell, paper cross-stitch sachet, 92.

Susan Z. Douglas, knitted Santa, 45.

Patti Engelbrecht, Nordic-design duplicate-stitch sweater and woodburned tray and coasters, 88.

Joyce M. Gillis, puppy wreath, 49; elf, 64.

Joan Green, cross-stitch sled ornaments, 66.

Barb Griffin, gingerbread house welcome sign, 55; reindeer basket, 50; Kris and Mrs. Kringle, 70; bear, 72; nightshirt, 76.

Linda Hendrickson, baby bunting, 77.

Polly Henry, stuffed puppy, 86.

Julie Ingleman and Marilyn Ginsburg, tulip door basket, 38.

Doxie A. Keller, decorated sweatshirts, 82.

Jo S. Kittinger, Dip 'N Drape ruffled wreath, 58.

Carol Krob, beaded bag and ornaments, 36.

Hannia Moore, paper-cutout greeting cards, 35; place mats, 68.

Sandra K. Ramey, rush wreath, 69.

Walter Rush, construction of reindeer and cardinal lawn decorations, 44.

Barbara Steele, corn husk Santa, 40.

Nan Tournier, lace-snowflake tree skirt, 63.

Carole Trapani, ski bunny, 60.

The Vanessa-Ann Collection, white tree skirt with hearts, 52.

Suzanne Wall, lamb patchwork stocking, 46.

Janice Weinstein, stitching of duplicate-stitch sweater, 88.

Eileen Westfall, "Santa Lives Here" wall hanging, 48; hot mitt, 93.

Lois Winston, cross-stitch sampler tray, 34; mouse card holder, 51; "Daddy's Little Angel" cross-stitch sweatshirt, 85.

PHOTOGRAPHERS

Jim Bathie, 41, 109, 111.

Gary Clark, 1, 7, 8-9, 10, 11, 12, 13, 14, 15, 26, 27, 28, 29, 34, 37, 38, 45, 46, 48, 51, 57, 58, 65, 68, 70, 72, 80, 90, 92, 93.

Steve Cridland, 22, 23, 24, 25.

Colleen Duffley, cover, 35, 42-43, 44, 49, 50, 55, 63, 66, 67, 69, 76, 77, 84, 86, 91, 94-95, 96, 98, 100, 102-103, 104, 107, 114, 115, 117, 119, 120, 121, 123, 126-127.

Bob Hawkes, 18-19, 20, 21.

Mary-Gray Hunter, 53, 54.

Beth Maynor, 2-3, 4, 5, 6, 33.

John O'Hagan, 30-31, 32.

Mary Carolyn Pindar, 16, 17.

Melissa Springer Rogers, 60.

Cheryl Sales, 74-75, 78-79, 83, 85, 88, 89.

PHOTOSTYLISTS

Leslie Byars, 67.

Lee D. Chapman, 45, 72, 90.

Kay Clarke, 94-95, 96, 98, 100, 102-103, 104, 107, 109, 111, 114, 115, 117, 119, 120, 121, 123, 126-127.

Connie Formby, 53, 54, 74-75.

Nancy Ingram, 18, 20, 21.

Karen Rogers, 86, 94-95, 96, 98, 100, 102-103, 104, 107.